THE ST. ELIZABETH HOSPITAL FIRE IN IOWA

BRET GRIMES

THE History PRESS

Published by The History Press
Charleston, SC
www.historypress.com

First published 2024

Manufactured in the United States

ISBN 9781467155571

Library of Congress Control Number: 2023945828

CONTENTS

Acknowledgements 5

1. Before the Blaze 9
2. Breaking Ground 19
3. A Vulnerable Population 25
4. An Eerie Omen 29
5. J.W.E. 36
6. The First Alarm 43
7. Soaked in Water 56
8. Filled to Capacity 63
9. Tick Tock 79
10. Confession 85
11. Back Behind Iron Bars 93
12. A Fireproof Future 99
13. More Than Just Names 105

Bibliography 123
Index 125
About the Author 128

ACKNOWLEDGEMENTS

I owe a great debt of gratitude to a number of people in my life without whom this book would never have made it into your hands. To my wonderful and supportive wife, editor and chief motivator, thanks for pushing me through some of the challenges that are present in a project like this. Without you, this book never would have made it to this point. To my sweet kids, who loved the idea of their dad writing a book and being in a bookstore—I hope Daddy made you proud.

To my friend Aaron Mack, who has shared as much enthusiasm for the project as I have, I greatly appreciate all your advice and insight. They were vital to take this book from an idea to a reality. To Cody Jaeger with the Davenport Fire Museum and Katie Reinhardt with the Special Collections Department at the Davenport Public Library, thank you for the work that you put in to bring this history to life. You will never fully understand the impact that you made.

To Roy Porter, the only fireman who helped fight this tragedy who is still alive, thank you for your willingness to retell your story to me—I hope I did it justice. And to Chad Rhoad, The History Press and Arcadia Publishing, thank you for believing in this story.

Lastly, to you, the reader—thank you for keeping history alive. My goal was always to preserve the story and those who were involved. That is only possible with you sharing this piece of history with others. Thank you for your passion.

At 2:06 a.m. on Saturday, January 7, 1950, the Davenport Fire Department responded to an alarm which was destined to ring throughout the world. The operator made the announcement for which the Fire Department had been waiting, with dread in their hearts, for many years: "St. Elizabeth's Mental ward in the rear of Mercy Hospital."

—Davenport fire chief Lester Schick

CHAPTER 1

BEFORE THE BLAZE

January 7, 1950, was supposed to be another ordinary day. The events of that day were not supposed to be recalled by hundreds and later testified to under oath, in front of a jury. It wasn't supposed to be a day where lives were taken and those spared were left sculpted and manipulated into something unrecognizable. It wasn't supposed to be a day that would overrun funeral homes, attract media attention across the globe and leave siblings arguing as they tried to identify the remains of their loved one. As it turns out, Saturday, January 7, 1950, was not just another ordinary day. In fact, it was one of the worst days in history for a small community situated on the Mississippi River and one that, in many ways, would shape and affect history forever.

At St. Elizabeth's psychiatric ward on the campus of Mercy Hospital in Davenport, Iowa, the afternoon began winding down. Fifty-seven-year-old Stella Nawrocki, of East Moline, Illinois, stepped out of the halls of the facility and into the cold January air accompanied by her husband. John Nawrocki was happy to have his wife back at his side, after having been without her for a number of weeks while she received treatment for her mental illness. John was a shear operator at International Harvester—a hardworking Polish immigrant who had moved to the Quad Cities with his wife after getting married in Chicago, Illinois, twelve years earlier.

Together they strolled on, hand in hand, toward their car, with their backs turned to the brick facade of St. Elizabeth's psychiatric ward. Certainly, they couldn't have imagined that those very bricks would come tumbling to the

St. Elizabeth's in the summer of 1949, just months before it was destroyed in the fire. *Photo courtesy of the Davenport Public Library.*

ground a matter of hours later. Stella smiled at her husband as he opened her door to the car, unaware that being discharged now would save her life. A few feet away, back inside the brick building, sixty-three other patients, mostly women, carried on with their afternoon. One of them, twenty-two-year-old Elnora Epperly, wandered the hallways, eagerly anticipating her release the next day.

Dr. Werner Hollander, a local psychiatrist, entered the building through the same door and prepared to visit his six patients who were currently seeking treatment at the mental institution: Marie Applegate, Flossie Thayer, Elnora Epperly, Amy Rivers, Betty Loeding and Lola Strine. These patients varied in severity of symptoms and diagnosis, with most suffering from some subtype of schizophrenia or manic depression. That day, while at the hospital administering treatment to his patients, Dr. Hollander would perform both deep insulin shock therapy and electrical shock therapy to those patients in his care. Dr. Hollander had an extensive background in neurology and found that patients responded well to these two types of treatment. He wasn't the only one—physicians all around the world used these two therapies as standard protocols to treat various mental health conditions.

"Years ago, we thought that personality was something static, but we now know that it can be altered," Dr. Hollander explained to a room full of Davenport schoolteachers in 1948. Specifically referring to those he treated at St. Elizabeth's on the first Friday in January, he mentioned that these patients "believed that [they] were responsible for all of the trouble in the world" and that this was a result of the development of someone who was an "introvert and lacked self-confidence." Dr. Hollander believed that individuals could have their personalities permanently altered with these therapies, forever improving their prognosis. Today, we understand that the treatments once used by Dr. Hollander, such as electric shock and deep insulin coma therapy, did indeed often improve patients' conditions—some estimates suggesting at least 75 percent of the time. While the efficacy of these types of treatments was well supported, it could be argued that they walked the thin line between ethical and unethical by today's standards.

After spending a few hours in the hospital on Friday, Dr. Hollander left and returned to his private practice, located in the Davenport Bank building in downtown Davenport. It was a relatively new practice, having only opened its doors to patients two years prior. Then again, Dr. Hollander himself was a relatively new physician, as well. Prior to moving to Davenport, he practiced at the state mental health institution in Mount Pleasant, Iowa, for ten months. He was a German immigrant who attended medical school in Switzerland prior to moving to the United States. He worked as an internal medicine resident physician in Alabama and then completed further training in New York State. Dr. Hollander was well respected during his short time in Davenport because he practiced both neurology and psychiatry. He cared for a number of challenging patients, primarily women, children and young adults. He also frequently gave speeches within local organizations in an attempt to combat the development of mental health problems and help parents better understand their children's behavior. It was his belief that early detection and correction could curb the symptoms of mental illness.

As Dr. Hollander left Mercy hospital that day, he expected to return to see his patients the following week, on Monday. However, after the unfolding of unforeseen events, Dr. Hollander would return only a number of hours later—this time arriving with more haste than he left with. Some of his time there that night would be spent treating those who survived; other parts of that time would be spent identifying patients of his who had been left nearly unrecognizable.

Another prominent Davenport physician, Dr. John H. Sunderbruch, left his private medical practice in downtown Davenport on Friday evening and took the drive north to St. Elizabeth's psychiatric ward to do rounds on his patients. Dr. Sunderbruch was a one-of-a-kind guy, the type of family physician that patients dream of. He practiced with a great bedside manner, building personal connections with his patients, and most importantly, he was always equipped with the latest medical information available. When he spoke, his patients listened. One of his friends would later recount that he "treated the whole person, not just the ailment."

After rounding at St. Elizabeth's, Dr. Sunderbruch returned to his wife and four children at his home west of downtown Davenport. After eating dinner and helping with the children, John retired to bed early. Not only was he tired from a long day of tending to patients, but he also felt as if he was coming down with some sort of respiratory illness.

Dr. Sunderbruch was as much of an asset to the Davenport community as one could be. He spent the majority of his medical career serving as the city physician, helping guide healthcare decision-making in the city. The city physician assisted in the building of new facilities and made recommendations about legislation that affected health, such as licensing, permitting and testing of dairy facilities and anything else that would directly impact the health of the community. Not only did he care for patients privately, but he played a large role in caring for the public, too—seeing that the community was well taken care of. When not serving the greater community, he served patients in the private practice he cofounded, the Davenport Clinic, a practice that still exists today.

Dr. Sunderbruch was a devout Catholic and active member of St. Mary's Church. He was also a retired army captain, having served his country in World War II as an army physician, attending to soldiers who fought in the Pacific Theater in the Indian Ocean. After retiring from the military, he served as president or vice president of almost every local organization imaginable—including the United Way, the chamber of commerce, the Center for Active Seniors, Inc. (CASI) and the Scott County Board of Health. He was also the first surgeon in the Quad Cities to perform open heart surgery.

With all his community involvement and service, it is no wonder Dr. Sunderbruch was one of the desperately needed leaders on January 7, 1950. He heard his phone ringing around two fifteen on that cold January night. Without hesitation, John answered the phone. It was a relative of his who lived on West Rusholme Street, a block or so east of St. Elizabeth's.

"Hello?" the half-dazed physician said.

"Jack, hey. Jack, you there? Hey, I think Mercy Hospital is on fire," his relative told him.

Sitting up in bed, Dr. Sunderbruch hung up the receiver and felt his pupils dilate and his heart begin to race. Unsurprisingly, John was also a member of the Davenport Second Alarmers, the volunteer fire association. The popular physician apparently wasn't fond of spare time. John picked the phone back up and dialed the number for the Davenport Police Department—a place he knew well, having worked frequently with the police in his capacities within the city. He wanted to know if the report of Mercy Hospital being on fire was true, and the officer who picked up confirmed that indeed it was, and the fire was specifically located at the mental health facility known as St. Elizabeth's. Dr. Sunderbruch ran to his closet, quickly got himself dressed and was heading for the door when the phone rang again, this time regarding his day job. It was the Physicians and Surgeons Exchange, requesting his services at the hospital. They had no idea that he was already on his way out the door to fulfill his volunteer firefighter duties or that he had already spoken to the police. Dr. Sunderbruch told them that he was on his way and continued his hustle toward the door, into his car and across town to the psychiatric ward, St. Elizabeth's.

Part-time physician and part-time fireman John Sunderbruch pulled down the alley behind his home at 2246 West Third Street and headed north toward the hospital. It was a ten-minute drive from his residence to the facility. John knew this route well, as he had made the drive hundreds of times over the years to round on and care for his patients. As his taillights faded into the deep black of the cold night, the Sunderbruchs' telephone rang one more time. It was the Second Alarmers—they needed John's help, too.

St. Elizabeth's psychiatric ward was a staple for mental health care in the Davenport community. At the time of the tragedy, patients had been receiving treatment there for almost eighty years. The facility managed thousands of primarily female patients who presented with varying symptoms and diagnoses. Almost all the patients there were inpatient, meaning that they lived at St. Elizabeth's for a period of time while they received treatment. Most of these women would be there for a matter of weeks before being released—either after enough improvement was achieved or when no progress was being made and another method of treatment and facility needed to be sought.

There was a third category of patients at St. Elizabeth's; these women were known as "life-long residents." Some of these were patients who had come to St. Elizabeth's of their own volition and continued receiving treatment or care from the facility for the remainder of their lives. Others were committed by their families, requiring the families to pay large sums of money to keep them in treatment permanently. These were oftentimes older women who had no spouses or children and had lived with relatives before entering St. Elizabeth's. Without much in the way of a social or home life, these women were more inclined to stay as permanent residents at St. Elizabeth's than those with families or children.

St. Elizabeth's was a private institution, similar to most healthcare facilities today. This means that most of the patients were admitted on the recommendation of their family physician, like Dr. Sunderbruch, or their psychiatrist, like Dr. Hollander. A few of the patients were brought there by recommendation of the State of Iowa, but these were relatively rare. Most state-initiated patients would have sought treatment at the state facility in Mount Pleasant, Iowa, rather than St. Elizabeth's.

The mental health facility stood in the middle of the area that constituted the campus of Mercy Hospital. It was the only local mental health facility that was associated with a hospital, making it sought after for its high level of care. On the southeast corner of the block, near the intersection of Lombard Street and Marquette Street, was the main hospital building. It was a large *T*-shaped facility, with six stories rising almost ninety feet into the air in the center of the building. It was flanked on either side by five-story sections that transitioned into four-story sixty-foot sections on either side. This section of the hospital was made almost entirely out of concrete and tile, leading to its designation as a fireproof facility.

Behind the main facility stood a number of large attached additions, each added on as the demand and technology of the hospital changed. North of the main hospital building stood the nurses' home, to the east of the campus, and St. Elizabeth's, to the west. Approximately one hundred feet to the west of St. Elizabeth's stood St. John's psychiatric ward, the male counterpart to St. Elizabeth's. Tucked behind St. Elizabeth's were the steam laundry and boiler room facilities.

St. Elizabeth's was a brick building, with much of its original construction from the early 1870s intact. It, too, had received a number of additions and improvements over the years and at capacity could hold around eighty patients and staff. The interior of the building was mostly wooden—not fireproof, like the main hospital building. The brick building stood three and a half stories tall, with its basement partially sunken into the ground. It had twelve-inch-thick brick outer walls and, at its center, stood over thirty

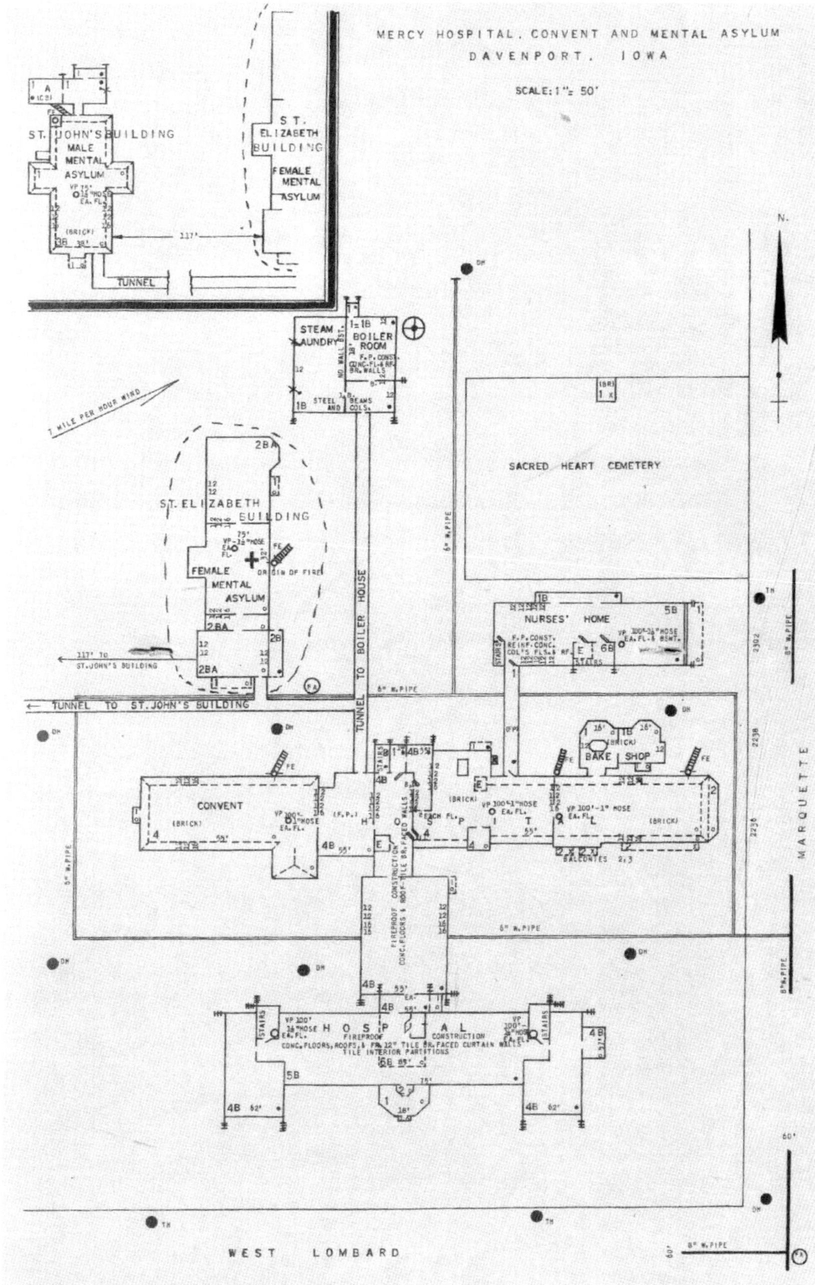

This map of the Mercy campus produced by the Iowa Inspection Bureau shows St. Elizabeth's location compared to other properties nearby. *Photo courtesy of the Davenport Fire Museum.*

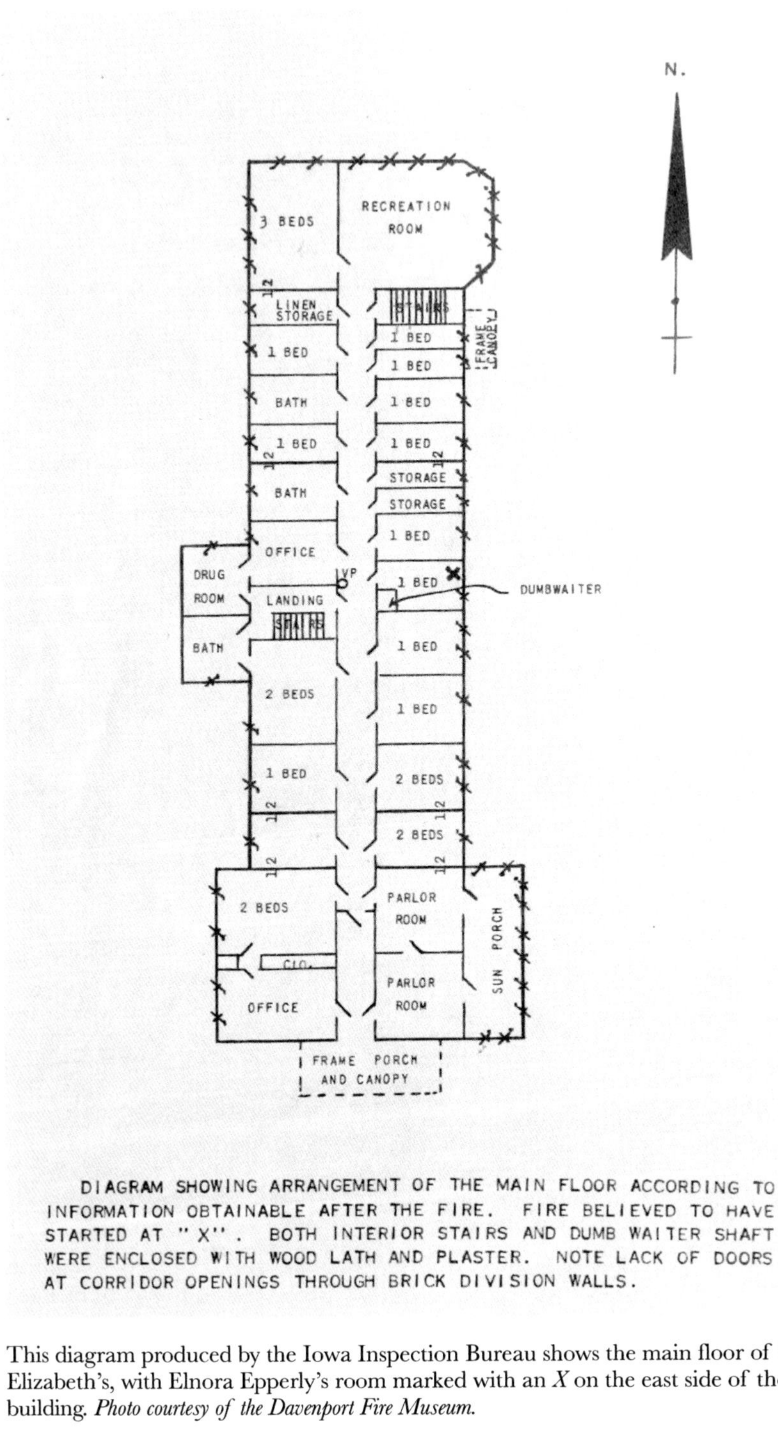

This diagram produced by the Iowa Inspection Bureau shows the main floor of St. Elizabeth's, with Elnora Epperly's room marked with an *X* on the east side of the building. *Photo courtesy of the Davenport Fire Museum.*

feet high. Altogether, the area of the building was just shy of twenty-five thousand feet, a large facility for its purposes. St. Elizabeth's was the larger building of the two psychiatric wards on Mercy Hospital's campus.

Almost every window on the outside of the facility was securely barred by iron "heavy wire grilles." These consisted of iron rods, placed four inches apart, running vertically up and down the window frame, anchored by three flat horizontal bars that held the vertical bars in place. These horizontal bars were fastened by large screws that anchored them into the structure of the building. There was only one exception to this type of arrangement, and that was a window on the west side of the building that did have iron bars but was equipped with a hinge and clasp locking mechanism. This window played a critical role in the rescue efforts that took place on January 7, 1950.

There were two entrances to the facility, the main one being the stairs and porch to the south, with a smaller, less traveled set of stairs and porch on the northern half of the east side. On the east side of the building, between these two entrances, was the building's lone fire exit. Technically, there was one additional access point to the facility—the tunnel underneath it. During construction, Mercy elected to have a tunnel system established, which adjoined the main hospital to both St. Elizabeth's and St. John's as well as the laundry facility. Most of the traffic in these tunnels was made up of hospital staff, transferring things like food and laundry from one facility to the next; the tunnels were rarely used by patients.

Inside the building stood two stair shafts, each traveling from the basement floor to the top floor. One of these was in the back of the building, at the northeast corner, near the lesser-used entrance. The other was in the center of the building on the west side of the hallway, next to an office. As a security measure, to keep patients on their assigned floors, the doors to these stair shafts were locked at night.

The building was not equipped with any fire-detecting devices or an automatic sprinkler system, both of which were widely used in commercial buildings in this period. In fact, two years prior, the fire department had recommended that an automatic sprinkler system be installed, but those in charge were greatly misinformed regarding the effectiveness of such devices. Inside the two stair shafts were cabinets with chemical fire extinguishers, standpipes that supplied water and water hoses that were to be used in case of an emergency. The doors to these cabinets remained locked at all times.

There also was no known evacuation plan organized for residents in case of emergency. With the constant turnover of patients in the facility, any practicing of this plan would have been rather difficult and potentially unsuccessful. This is all without mentioning that there were very few employees in the building, especially at night, when most patients were sleeping.

St. Elizabeth's had a total of fourteen employees on staff and only two working during the night and early morning hours of January 7, 1950—nurse Anna Neal and nurse's aide Josephine O'Toole. The likelihood of these two women being able to execute any sort of evacuation plan that involved sixty-three mentally ill patients was low. When also considering Neal's physical limitations (she was known for walking with a bad limp), executing such a plan might have been next to impossible.

To the east of St. Elizabeth's and directly behind the nurses' home sat the Sacred Heart Cemetery. This area, also owned by the Sisters of Mercy, was a burial ground for Sisters who had devoted their lives to the Catholic Church. It would later become the burial ground for some of those who lost their lives in the tragedy at St. Elizabeth's. This property, to this day, is still owned by the Sisters of Mercy Catholic organization.

CHAPTER 2

BREAKING GROUND

On the banks of the Mississippi River where the river turns west stood Davenport, Iowa, a sprawling community working to recover in the shadows of the American Civil War. Prior to the onset of the Civil War, this river town with a population of around fifteen thousand was booming, at a crossroads of American travel both by boat and railroad. Vegetable crops like corn and soybeans and meats like pork and beef, along with other commodities, were shipped to places up and down America's largest river. The area thrived in its midwestern ways: hard work, humility and kindness.

By the summer of 1861, Davenport's bluffs were home to Camp McClellan—a military camp that housed over three thousand soldiers and later imprisoned upward of three hundred American Indians following the Minnesota Massacre. By this time, the city was playing an important part in the welfare of the United States by way of both exports from the area and military usage. The utilization of the Rock Island Arsenal, on a three-mile-long island situated between Iowa and Illinois, also added to the region's luster. These combining forces created a growing area in the mid- to late 1860s, and this growth created the need to support the community. Among the greatest needs that became evident was the need for a new hospital.

The story of that hospital begins in 1809 on a twenty-two-acre estate in northeast Dublin, Ireland, in a mansion called the Coolock House. It was there that Mr. and Mrs. William Callaghan, a wealthy Protestant and Quaker couple, housed Sister Catherine McAuley, who served as their household manager and companion to Mrs. Catherine Callaghan. McAuley served the Callaghan family faithfully for twenty years, growing in her own Catholic faith and witnessing the Callaghans' generosity. On the death of William on November 10, 1829, her tireless dedication was rewarded, as she became the sole residuary legatee of his estate and life's savings, valued at the time at £25,000 (equal to nearly 3.8 million USD today).

Sister Catherine took her appetite for caring for the poor and needy, which was now fueled with enough funding to bring her ideas to life, and established the Sisters of Mercy in Dublin, Ireland, on December 12, 1831. She vowed, along with two others, to devote her life to "the Sisters of Mercy, established for the visitation of the sick poor, and protection and instruction of poor females." This convent soon grew to establish branches throughout both Ireland and England.

Years later, in 1843, while traveling to the convent in Carlow, Ireland, Reverend M. O'Conner pleaded with the Sisters of Mercy for their help at his diocese in Pittsburgh, Pennsylvania. The region was growing, and the need for good Catholic schools in his community had become apparent. Seven sisters answered the call and traveled back to the United States with him, first arriving in New York City on December 10, 1843. Once there, they were greeted by Reverend William Quarter, bishop-elect of the Chicago diocese. He, too, needed dedicated missionaries, as he was trying to mold the thriving and quickly growing community of Chicago, Illinois. He wanted to develop schools and programs for the rich, the poor, the young and the old and knew he could not do it alone. Bishop Quarter pleaded with the Sisters of Mercy for their help. They responded that while they couldn't help immediately, they eventually could—and shortly thereafter, in September 1846, five Sisters arrived in Chicago to start what would become St. Xavier's Academy.

Among those who left Pittsburgh and traveled to Chicago were Mother Mary Elizabeth Borromeo Johnson and Mother Mary Francis Monholland. When they arrived, they were trained by staff at Rush Medical Center, and they would go on to open Mercy Chicago in 1850. Eleven years later, as the country turned its attention to the battlefield, the Chicago Sisters of Mercy assisted in aiding and treating soldiers during the Civil War. The Chicago Sisters of Mercy, in all their humility, won the trust and respect of their peers—and, most notably, the trust of the United States government. This respect and support is best embodied in this letter written on their behalf:

To whom it may concern:

On application of the Sisters of Mercy of Chicago, furnish such provisions as they desire to purchase and charge the same to the War Department.

Abraham Lincoln

On the conclusion of the war in 1865, Mother Borromeo and four others traveled west in an attempt to start the first Mercy Foundation west of the Mississippi River. Their chosen destination was the small town of DeWitt, Iowa, where they planned to open an "Academy for Girls."

Following the conclusion of the Civil War, the United States began fighting another domestic threat, this one doing damage to cities much more quickly. It was the extremely contagious bacteria that caused cholera. This disease would spread through cities and communities like wildfire, as it was easily transmitted through drinking water and poor sanitation habits. Once contracted, it left patients in severe pain, causing diarrhea and vomiting within hours of onset. Many of these patients died from the disease, and others were left withered and broken. Cholera became incredibly difficult to manage in communities in the mid- to late 1800s, and by the summer of 1873, it had reached the river town of Davenport, Iowa.

In Davenport, as the cholera pandemic raged on, the city's board of health created a makeshift 250-bed hospital inside a warehouse downtown to secure a place to treat community members who had contracted the illness. Within a few hours of its establishment, the Scott County Poor Farm (as it was later called) had all 250 beds filled with critically ill patients. Due to the urgency and the overwhelming need experienced at the makeshift hospital, the board of health did not have enough staff to attend to the sick patients.

Hearing of these conditions in Davenport, only twenty-five miles south of DeWitt, the Sisters of Mercy offered their help. Having been trained both in the halls of Rush Medical Center and on the battlefields of the Civil War, three Sisters of Mercy made the trip down to Davenport to see the conditions for themselves and offer their help and expertise. One of these Sisters was forty-one-year old Sister Mary Elizabeth Borromeo Johnson.

It was during that trip south to Davenport, Iowa, that Sister Borromeo observed the horrific conditions at the Scott County Poor Farm and realized the need a community of this size had for a hospital with adequately trained staff. Armed with both her background as a nurse in the Civil War and her experiences among hospital personnel in Chicago, and knowing she could rely on the help of the Sisters of Mercy, she knew she would be capable of making this a reality. When joining the Sisters of Mercy, she had vowed to care for the "sick, poor, and ignorant," and she knew she had to live up to those vows. After four weeks of caring for the needy in Davenport, Sister Borremeo and the Sisters of Mercy returned to Dewitt to continue the development of the academy for girls.

On a return trip to Davenport to help fundraise for the girls' school in Dewitt, Sister Borromeo returned again to the Scott County Poor Farm and met with its director, Charles Watkins. While there, she again witnessed the neglect and the lack of appropriate care given to the sick and afflicted in this community. There were critically ill patients out in the open air, pregnant patients intermixed with those with contagious diseases and even mentally ill patients shackled and chained to their beds as a way of containing them. The city was growing—at this point, the census recorded nearly twenty thousand people—and the community was desperate for help. Watkins pleaded with Sister Borromeo, and she graciously answered his plea. A hospital was to be built in Davenport, and the care and treatment of patients would greatly improve once heightened to the standards set by the Sisters of Mercy.

Around this time, in the late 1860s, a vacant building sat in the countryside north of Davenport, Iowa. This rural structure, which had remained mostly vacant since 1857, previously housed the Academy of the Immaculate Conception, an all-girls school that would eventually move to a more central location—Eighth and Main Street, near downtown Davenport—to provide easier travel for its students.

A listing published in the *Davenport Daily Gazette* on March 7, 1865, described the ten-acre lot on the northern border of town as "beautiful in its natural condition" and "tastefully laid out." While the city of Davenport had grown, much of its population was still centered near the downtown area. In fact, the ten-acre property described in the *Davenport Daily Gazette* was just outside the Davenport city limits, excusing the new purchasers from being subject to city taxes. The original building, which stood in good condition, cost $9,000 and included a nearby barn.

Sister Borromeo spent the next year working on the project and met with the Scott County Board of Supervisors late in 1869 in an effort to secure a property for the hospital. Revered Catholic priest Father J.A. Palamourgues suggested that the School of the Immaculate Conception and its land be used to fulfill the need for a new hospital. In her meetings with the county board, Sister Borromeo requested that the property be donated instead of purchased. In a letter to Scott County dated October 14, 1869, she wrote,

"Our main objective will be relief of suffering in all its forms—not as a general speculation or for a profit, but that it may prove a general public benefit." The board of supervisors replied to Sister Borremeo with the following statement given at their meeting on October 13, 1869:

> *The Sisters of Mercy are willing to open an institution and include their plans, the care of the poor and insane of Scott County. The general purpose of the institution is to include every class of suffering, except contagion.*

The Sisters of Mercy were awarded the ten acres of land, including the building, by the county board of supervisors. The county also agreed to advance the hospital a loan of $2,000 toward transforming the facility from its original condition as a school and helping it operate as a hospital. The Sisters of Mercy were also given an adjoining ten-acre lot that was previously owned by the widow of the late Judge G.C.R. Mitchell, who was a philanthropic supporter of the Catholic Church.

In December 1869, the *Davenport Morning Democrat* described the property as consisting of a "fine, large brick building, surrounded by fine groves of fruit and forest trees, together with twenty acres of ground." It also was advertised as including a mineral spring that "possesses medical virtues not generally known to the residents of our city."

Finally, in 1870, the letters of incorporation were drafted, and the Sisters of Mercy and Mother Mary Borromeo opened Mercy Hospital. Sister Borromeo was happy, the City of Davenport was happy and together, they both looked forward to the future of better healthcare and better conditions for the deserving citizens of this region.

Two years after opening Mercy Hospital, Mother Borromeo continued her advocacy for the sick and afflicted, particularly women, and in 1872, Mercy Hospital opened the St. Elizabeth's psychiatric ward for women—named after Mother Borromeo, whose given name at birth was Elizabeth. The standalone building was four stories tall and sat about one hundred yards from the main building of Mercy Hospital. Prior to 1872, patients who were mentally ill received treatment in the main hospital quarters. Having separate quarters allowed treatment to be given more efficiently and prevented those who had more verbal struggles from affecting others in the hospital.

While her legacy would live forever, her life would be cut short. On September 2, 1874, Mother Mary Elizabeth Johnson Borromeo succumbed to cancer at the very hospital she helped bring to life. She was buried on the east side of the hospital campus, on the very land she found less than ten years prior. Her remains rest there, covered by a white chapel and accompanied by a stone cross that reads:

> *To the Memory of Rev. Mother Mary Borromeo Superior of the Convent Of Our Lady of Mercy Davenport Who Departed This Life Sept. 2, 1874 Age 42 Years Requiescat in Pace*

In the years following Mother Borromeo's death, Mercy Hospital continued to grow and flourish as a greatly respected healthcare facility in eastern Iowa. In 1880, Mercy completed an addition on St. Elizabeth's psychiatric ward; in 1883, the first documented appendectomy in the United States was recorded; and in 1884, St. John's Hospital for Mentally Ill Men opened on Mercy's campus. In 1886, a nearby building called the Magdalen Hospital for Wayward Girls was torn down (after only ten years of housing unwed new mothers), and the space was used to build an addition to St. Elizabeth's. This increased the capacity of the mental ward building to eighty patients.

As the community grew, so did Mercy hospital, and with the population climbing to around thirty thousand in 1895, St. Luke's Hospital, a sister facility to Mercy, was opened in downtown Davenport. This allowed for more convenient healthcare for those residents living closer to the city center. This was particularly impactful because travel was still by horse and buggy.

Mercy's footprint in the community would continue to expand, with the campus adding a man-made lake in 1907 (it would be removed seven years later) and a large structural addition in 1932 with 150 beds, a surgery department, a pediatric wing, an X-ray facility and a laboratory. All this growth, expansion and success would come to a screeching halt in the early morning hours of January 7, 1950.

CHAPTER 3

A VULNERABLE POPULATION

The care given to people who suffered from mental health disorders in 1950 varied somewhat from the way their disorders are treated at the present time. It would be difficult to fully understand the tragedy and significance of the fire at the St. Elizabeth's psychiatric ward without understanding the stigma against those suffering from mental illnesses and, in particular, how these patients were treated in eastern Iowa. In the period leading up to the fire at St. Elizabeth's, the building was referred to as a "female insane asylum." This information is not presented to impose some sort of penalty or shame on those who use such language but to help the reader understand that this was simply the terminology used during this time. People suffering from mental illnesses were considered "sick," and the expectation was that they should be housed somewhere else until they could receive enough treatment to be "cured" and return to normal society. The word *cured* here is used purposefully.

Schizophrenia was first defined in the late 1800s by the German psychiatrist Emil Kraepelin. He believed that these patients were suffering some form of dementia that resulted in hallucinations, depressive episodes, delusional manifestations, agitation and paranoia. He described this disease as having an early onset and a poor prognosis and producing clusters of both physical and psychological symptoms. He believed that this disease had a specific cause and affected the makeup of the human brain. He called this disease dementia praecox.

Kraepelin's theory that dementia praecox was a disease associated with an anomaly in the anatomy of the brain caused great challenges in finding a successful method of treatment. Most of the technology that is now used to study the details and intricacies of brain anatomy was not available to physicians treating mental health patients in the 1950s. CAT scans were not in use until the 1970s, and MRIs weren't available until 1984. This means that while researchers and medical professionals may have believed that schizophrenia was a result of abnormal development of the brain, this couldn't be proven in patients who were still living—making successful treatment rather difficult.

By 1911, Swiss psychiatrist Eugen Bleuler had devoted a great deal of time studying this disease and coined a new name to describe it, schizophrenia, which literally translates to "a mind that is torn asunder." Bleuler believed that instead of this disease being caused by the brain's anatomy, it had more to do with the processes of the brain and how it carries out tasks. This belief is important to the story about the St. Elizabeth's fire because it opened the door to possible treatment. Physicians began working with Bleuler's new theory that while the anatomy of the brain could not be changed, the brain's processes and patterns could be influenced. By minimizing or ridding patients of their brain dysfunction, psychiatrists believed they could cure them of this disease—or so their understanding of the disease led them to believe.

With or without a good understanding of the cause of schizophrenia, a number of treatment methods were initiated to try to "cure" patients of their condition. These included inducing fevers in patients with sulfur and oils, using electrical shock therapy and inducing comas in patients through high doses of insulin. The latter method, deep insulin coma therapy (DICT), was the most common treatment in the 1930–50s, both across the country and in the Quad Cities.

The St. Elizabeth's women's psychiatric ward was a critical asset for the Quad Cities. While it wasn't the only place for women seeking treatment of mental illness, it was the only one associated with a hospital. Therefore, St. Elizabeth's was utilized more than other independent facilities and frequently used for the most complex diagnoses and the most critical of patients.

Deep insulin coma therapy was developed by psychiatrist Manfred Sakel in the 1920s and quickly became widespread. Sakel had noticed that a patient he was treating for a morphine addiction curbed their habits after coming out of an insulin-induced coma. He deduced that this treatment could have clinical applications outside of addiction and began administering it to schizophrenic patients. Shortly thereafter, it was adopted and used as a primary treatment at St. Elizabeth's in Davenport.

The premise of insulin "shock" therapy, as it was sometimes called, was relatively simple. Patients were injected with high amounts of insulin, which greatly lowered their blood sugar until it caused them to enter a coma. Once the patient was in a coma, they would be left in that state for a period ranging from fifteen minutes to four hours. During this time, patients were completely unconscious, lacking any reflexes, pupil dilation or reactions to other stimuli. In some of the more extreme cases (this is not believed to have happened in the Quad Cities), physicians would also extract large amounts of cerebrospinal fluid from patients and replace it with air, believing that this would somehow improve their condition.

Patients who were receiving insulin shock therapy would undergo treatment for weeks or months, typically receiving treatment five or six days a week; this would typically occur until patients had been placed in a coma on fifty or sixty separate occasions. As the patient's body became less reactive to smaller doses, staff administered progressively larger and larger quantities of insulin. After the coma had lasted for the desired amount of time, staff brought the patient out of the coma by administering sugar to them, thereby raising their blood sugar levels and restoring consciousness. Once patients returned to consciousness, some reported feeling "reborn again."

Deep insulin coma therapy, which gained popularity in the late 1930s, was a staple in the treatment of schizophrenic patients until the early 1950s. Although by today's standards it may seem experimental or barbaric in nature, this treatment was widely accepted by clinicians and patients alike. Research at the time reported an improvement rate upward of 90 percent in patients who received insulin shock therapy. However, this would be proven inaccurate in the late 1950s. In fact, it is now understood that as many as 5 percent of patients died as a result of receiving insulin shock therapy, while other recipients were left with severe brain damage and obesity.

After receiving such therapies, patients would have to be monitored for an extended time due to some experiencing what were referred to as "after-shocks," during which they might slip back into a coma-like state caused by the induced hypoglycemia. Medical doctors would have to be available to help manage these patients when this occurred. This would prove to be a problem in an understaffed institution such as St. Elizabeth's. Other patients would report feeling "extremely restless" and in an excited or agitated state following treatment. To counteract this, residents at St. Elizabeth's who received insulin shock therapy were allowed to smoke freely in the building during daylight hours to help calm their nerves. The side effects caused by this therapy necessitated a greater than usual number of staff to help oversee patients receiving this treatment regimen.

An article in the *Quad City Times* on April 8, 1953, described how doctors were using "insulin shock therapy to help straighten out the mental illness of schizophrenia, or so called split-personality." However common and accepted the practice of insulin shock therapy was in the early 1950s, the side effects of treatment and the brittle nature of the patients receiving it would certainly increase the vulnerability of those patients when tragedy struck on the night of January 7, 1950.

CHAPTER 4

AN EERIE OMEN

The 1940s, a memorable decade, was drawing to a close, and the 1950s was quickly approaching. The voices of Bing Crosby and Nat King Cole emanated from the radio, James Dean showed up for the first time on television screens in a Pepsi Cola commercial and the United States was prepared for better and more lucrative days ahead. President Harry Truman was delicately guiding the country out of the sights of the Great Depression and past the scars of World War II, tiptoeing around an armed conflict with the Soviet Union.

Meanwhile, in the growing river town of Davenport, Iowa, life was in many ways both simple and exciting. Color televisions made their way into homes, Slinkys tumbled their way down flights of stairs and Frisbees flew through backyards. Davenport's Municipal Stadium for baseball and football had just undergone an expansion project, the Capitol Theatre was the locals' choice for entertainment and the Aluminum Company of America (ALCOA) had built a new rolling mill in nearby Riverdale—the largest aluminum rolling plant in the United States.

The *Daily Times* newspaper rolled warm off the press, rather inconspicuously, on the afternoon of Friday, January 6, 1950. A copy of the *Daily Times* cost readers only a nickel to purchase. The front page was headlined "Truman Predicts Jobs for More Millions," as the fifth-year president looked to bolster the national economy. On a local level, the *Times* reported, Davenport mayor Arthur R. Kroppach had announced his candidacy for reelection, citing major growth in the city of Davenport as one of the strong selling points on his résumé. Other stories were about the company president of International Harvester Co. visiting local Quad City plants, Petersen's department store of Davenport holding a sale on Colonial beds for $19.95 and thirty-four-year-old actor Kirk Douglas and his wife, Diana Dill, announcing that they were getting a divorce. In every sense of the phrase, it was a slow news day as the first week of January came to a close.*

Twenty-two-year-old fireman Darrell Doss went to bed on Friday night hoping to get a full night of sleep, but he knew, realistically, that this was never a guarantee. It was the sixth of January, 1950, and the first week of the New Year was coming to an end. Holiday parties were over, Christmas decorations would soon be coming down and the New Year had begun. The Iowa winter, which is known to be unforgiving, was hitting its stride, with overnight temperatures hovering in the teens and very windy conditions. As a member of Truck Company No. 3 out of Davenport's downtown district, Doss knew that winter conditions in Iowa led to more fire emergency calls as residents sought creative ways to stay warm. The colder it got, the busier they would be—and the less sleep he would get. Doss didn't shy away from the challenge; in fact, he was accustomed to challenges. He was a military veteran, a marine, who had served his country in the South Pacific just a few years earlier, during World War II. He was a no-nonsense guy, loyal to the bone, who took care of his firemen and enjoyed protecting his community. He hadn't signed up for the job with any fear of hard work or lack of sleep. But, military training aside, nothing could have prepared him for the call he would receive a couple of hours after falling asleep—the call that would change his life forever.

Half a block to the north of Doss's home on Marquette Street stood a seventy-five-year-old four-story building that was ripe for disaster. A mere six months prior, the building had undergone some updating, including fresh paint, new wiring, varnishing of the wooden floors and a few other minor improvements. The building's aesthetics received the face lift they needed, but safety updates were not given the same priority. Despite

*John Nawrocki, whose wife, Stella, was released from St. Elizabeth's on Friday, January 6, 1950, before the fire, was featured in the paper the following day, January 7, 1950. On the second page of the *Daily Times*, the headline read, "Represent 173 Years with International Harvester Co.," with an accompanying picture of John Nawrocki, International Harvester Co. president J.L. McCaffrey and three other men. John was included in the picture as he was the longest tenured press department employee, having worked for the company forty-three years. His wife narrowly missed being part of the main story featured in the *Daily Times* that day: the St. Elizabeth's tragedy.

the Davenport Fire Department recommending, two years prior, that a sprinkler system be installed, budget restraints put that safety measure on hold once again.

One firefighter would later describe the building from firsthand experience. "[St. Elizabeth was] a big brick building, all wood inside," said Roy Porter in an interview with the *Quad City Times*. "Flammable furniture, old furniture. No smoke alarms. No fire extinguishers. And this is crucial—no sprinkler system." These oversights, combined with dry, windy winter weather, led to the perfect conditions for a fire to spread. All it needed was a source for ignition. Staff probably would have argued, however, that they took the measures necessary to keep the facility safe. In fact, while decorating for Christmas earlier that winter, they chose to not display a Christmas tree in the foyer. They believed that the lighted Christmas tree posed too much of a fire hazard for the facility and its residents.

Elnora Epperly of nearby Rock Island, Illinois, was one of the sixty-three residents of St. Elizabeth's psychiatric ward on the cold night of January 6, 1950. Earlier that evening, her husband, John Epperly, had come to visit and spend time with her. John adored his wife and looked after her closely. Even as she struggled with mental illness, John was patient and kind to her, always protective and doing his best to ensure she didn't experience unnecessary stress. Although Elnora was considered "comparatively normal" by hospital workers and oftentimes went home on the weekends to be with her husband, she stayed on campus that night. Around seven o'clock, Elnora and her husband played a couple hands of cards with residents Kenneth Melow and Lola Shrine. Closer to eight o'clock, William Super, a student at nearby St. Ambrose College and part-time orderly at St. Elizabeth's, stopped by Elnora's room while John was still visiting, and the three enjoyed conversation and a cigarette. As a recipient of insulin shock therapy, Elnora was given smoking privileges for symptom management. Super even borrowed Elnora's lighter, one she had originally intended as a wedding gift for her husband, with his initials—J.W.E.—inscribed on it.

Elnora was relatively new to the facility; she was admitted just over three weeks prior by her psychiatrist, Dr. Werner M. Hollander. He would later describe Elnora as an "acute patient," suggesting that her condition had worsened rather quickly, leading to the need for immediate treatment. Dr. Hollander diagnosed Elnora with schizophrenia, a mental health condition that causes impaired thoughts, hallucinations, delusions and odd behaviors. Dr. Hollander believed that this was secondary to some traumas Elnora had experienced.

Elnora Epperly is shown here in 1945, during her senior year, in the Rock Island High School yearbook, called the Watchman. *Photo courtesy of Rock Island High School.*

Elnora and her mother, Donna Carter, had been involved in a severe car accident on June 15, 1946, outside of Galesburg, Illinois. The car accident left forty-four-year-old Donna in a wheelchair and Elnora with severe head trauma. Since the accident, Elnora had felt a lot of guilt; she blamed herself for everything, including the poor condition the accident left her mother in. Mother and daughter were very close. Donna described Elnora as both "physically and mentally ill." On December 11, 1949, Elnora came to her mother complaining of a "splitting headache," and Elnora's coworkers at the insurance company Royal Neighbors in Rock Island said that she had been acting strangely all week. These two factors led John Epperly to seek medical attention for his wife, and on December 12, 1949, she was admitted to St. Elizabeth's psychiatric ward.

Donna also reported that Elnora was recently told by her physician that, because of her mental health difficulties and some physical impairments, it was unlikely that she would ever be able to conceive children and doctors considered her "sterile." For a young, twenty-two-year-old newlywed with dreams of starting a family, this was understandably a difficult burden to bear, and it caused a great deal of pain for Elnora.

Lucille Kalloway was one of the nurses' aides working the 3:00 p.m. to 11:00 p.m. shift that Friday evening and recalled having some difficulty with Elnora earlier that day. "She was a patient who was rather moody," Kalloway would later tell investigators.

> *You talked with her and she stood with an anxious expression on her face. She was occasionally concerned about other patients. While I was putting patients to bed at nine o'clock, she got into Mrs. Applegate's room, and kept saying, "It is a friend of mine. We want to visit."*
>
> *After convincing her that she couldn't visit at that time of night, I had to force her out of the room and into her own. She was getting Mrs. Applegate upset and excited. After she got in* [her room] *and I cleared out her room, she came out several times and would go out to the front door and back to the day room.*

When leaving Elnora's room, Kalloway took the box of Lucky Strike cigarettes, only a few still remaining, and grabbed a couple of matches that were scattered on her windowsill. There was no sign of a cigarette lighter in the room. Patients were allowed to smoke during the day, but matches and cigarettes were taken away from them at night.

On multiple occasions that night, Kalloway went back and forth with Elnora, finding her somewhere where she wasn't supposed to be, ushering her back to her room and then returning to her nursing duties. On one occasion, after Kalloway had a long talk with her, Elnora "promised" to stay in her room. After a few moments, she exited her room again and wandered to the north end of the building. The process continued; Kalloway was not unlike a parent bringing their young child back to their bedroom.

"I tried to tell her that she should get a good night's sleep; not to let anything bother her. She was rather confused. She kept frowning and saying, 'I don't get it. I don't get it. Why am I here?'" recalled Kalloway. It was later revealed that Elnora had undergone shock therapy earlier that day, possibly leading to some of her restlessness.

As it got closer to the end of her shift at eleven o'clock, Kalloway had to do her rounds on the upper floors and check on other patients. Realizing that she could not leave Elnora wandering around the second floor waking up other patients, Kalloway reached a conclusion.

"Finally, I had to lock her door," she would later testify to the state's attorney.

Elnora's room didn't have a lock and key closure; instead, a hook-and-eye latch secured on the outside of the doorframe was used to prevent her from future wanderings.

While by today's standards this may seem like an unusual and unethical practice, it was not uncommon at the time for patients being treated in mental health facilities to be locked in their rooms. The windows of St. Elizabeth's hospital were also secured, with iron bars running vertically down the window and crossing horizontally. Some of these windows could be unlocked with a key and opened from the outside; other windows were permanently secured, with bolts in all four corners of the windowsill. Keeping wandering mental health patients safely inside the facility was the number one priority every day that St. Elizabeth's was in operation.

On January 7, 1950, the number one priority soon became getting patients *out.*

Ten or fifteen minutes later, after completing her rounds on the upper floors, Lucille Kalloway returned to Elnora's room— Elnora hadn't left her mind. "Sometimes when patients are upset you can talk to them and relax them enough," she later recounted. She unlatched the door and entered Elnora's room, hoping to calm Elnora's nerves before ending her shift. She found Elnora sitting up at the end of her bed, so she helped her lie down, covered her up and asked, "Elnora, what's bothering you?"

Elnora replied, "Well, nothing. Just let me think." This was somewhat puzzling to Kalloway, so she continued, "Let's talk about it. Maybe you will feel better." But Elnora didn't want to talk, and at one point she even said to the concerned nurse's aide, "Let me alone—I want to think." Kalloway continued prying, but she wasn't able to get anything further from Elnora. She sincerely wanted to help, but Elnora wasn't giving her the option. In one final effort to calm her, Kalloway reminded Elnora that she was set to be discharged the next day and she should get a good night of sleep. She received no response.

Kalloway left Elnora Epperly's room after her best efforts to calm and reassure an obviously anxious and troubled young mind. After she closed the door, she paused and slid the hook into the eye of the latch.

There were two grisly indications of the horror that was soon to befall on this river town that, in retrospect, foretold the impending fire. While talking to investigators, Kalloway recalled that earlier on in the evening, "As I cleared her room of matches and cigarettes, Mrs. Epperly said to me, 'Well, I won't hurt anything.'" Did Elnora have plans to ignite the fire earlier in the evening, or was this just a schizophrenic patient experiencing a hallucination?

In hindsight, another startling prediction came from the fifty-five-year-old night supervisor and graduate nurse Anna Neal. Neal was a German immigrant who had worked at the hospital for a short while. She was short in stature, about five feet tall, and "a bit heavy set." She also walked with a noticeable limp, caused by a deformity in her left hip. Seasoned nurses tend to have a strong intuition about them, an indescribable quality that seems to increase their awareness of and response to certain events. Neal was reported to have the hobby of "fortune telling," and on Wednesday that week, just four days prior to the fire, she told W.F. Schmitt, a special attendant who was visiting someone in the hospital, that she "saw a big fire in the near future." This was corroborated by Myrtle

This portrait published in the newspaper shows Anna Neal, one of two St. Elizabeth employees working on the night of the fire. *Photo courtesy of the Daily Times.*

Baker of Davenport and two others who sat in a group with Neal on Sunday mornings studying the Bible and listening to her predictions of the future. They recalled that she had also predicted the election of Harry Truman, a fire at Rock Island High School and a tragic accident involving a young girl falling into a well.

CHAPTER 5

J.W.E

Around eleven o'clock on January 6, 1950, Kalloway was nearing the end of her shift when she realized that St. Elizabeth's was a bit short-staffed for the night shift. She decided to stop by and talk to Anna Neal, who would be the nurse working the 11:00 p.m. to 7:00 a.m. shift that night. Oftentimes, when there was a shortage of staff, it was Neal who would spend the night at the facility to help out. Recognizing the need for help, Kalloway offered to stay on duty but was met with a "huffy" response from Neal, who promised she could manage it alone. Kalloway obliged and left St. Elizabeth's when her shift concluded at eleven thirty.

Sometime around two o'clock in the morning, realizing she was locked in her second-story room and unable to sleep, Elnora Epperly took the lighter she had used to light her cigarette the evening before and set fire to a copy of the local newspaper, the *Rock Island Argus*. She then waved the flaming newspaper and lit the drapery covering her window on fire.[†]

Elnora now found herself in a dangerous situation and knew she had to evacuate her room. The blaze had taken off. Fire roared as it rushed up

---

† Elnora Epperly's reasoning for starting the fire was told many different ways, but what was widely accepted and repeated by investigators was that Elnora believed her husband was being beaten and abused and was possibly dead and the only way for her to signal for help and get herself out of the facility and back to him was to start a fire. Doctors would later suggest that Elnora was experiencing a hallucination that caused delusional thinking. They continued that if "her husband was killed, she would have no friends and would be taken away." Her husband, John, was not being beaten or abused. In fact, he wasn't even at the hospital. After visiting her earlier that evening, he left the facility at eight o'clock and returned home to 2346 5½ Avenue, Rock Island, Illinois, about four miles away.

the curtains like a rocket, sprawling toward the third floor above her. Once it settled into the wood, it spread outward in all directions. In the face of desperation, the twenty-two-year-old Elnora screamed, "*Fire! Fire! Help!*" and began pounding on the locked door. Neal, not far from Elnora's room, was awakened by her screams and rushed to Elnora's door. As she unlatched it, she could see a glow coming from the transom window above the doorframe. Neal threw the door open, and Elnora rushed past her.

As Neal opened the door to the rest of the building, the fire, like an animal chasing ferociously after its prey, followed the fresh source of oxygen and spread across the newly varnished wood toward the hallway. Before it reached the door, the fire found another source of fuel, the open dumbwaiter shaft, connecting all four floors, that was located in Elnora's room. Flames seeped into the opening and combusted up and down the open flue, following the source of fresh oxygen. Within a couple minutes of ignition, the fire had engulfed the room and begun spreading to all four floors. The other sixty-three people in the building were not yet aware of the rapidly growing, aggressive blaze.

Once Elnora exited her room, she took an immediate right and entered the unlocked room of her friend, Marilyn Beals, attempting to inform Beals of the fire. "I thought she would follow me out," Elnora later recalled. Beals never did, though, and was one of the first to die in the tragedy that night. Elnora then exited Marilyn's room and took a left toward the front of the building, where she was met with another locked door. Sitting next to the door, she found a chair, which she used to break the window in the upper half of the door, and she exited down the front stairs, throwing the lighter into a room before she left the building.

Josephine O'Toole, a nurse's aide and the only other St. Elizabeth's employee present that night, was awakened from her third-floor bed by screams coming from below her as the fire spread. O'Toole had been an employee of the psychiatric wing for about six and a half years, and while she wasn't actually on duty that night, she had taken up residence there full time. Her room was on the third floor, the level directly above the main floor, directly at the top of the stairs near the middle of the building. Combining her six and a half years of working at St. Elizabeth's with the fact that this was her full-time residence, nobody knew the building as well as she did.

O'Toole sat up in bed and listened. People causing commotion or yelling was not new or unusual at St. Elizabeth's—except at this time of night. As she sat there quietly, she wondered what time it was. Again, the muffled screams came from below, seemingly from outside the building. O'Toole

Assistant state fire marshal Adrian Lubberden points to the lighter used to start the fire that was found in the front foyer of St. Elizabeth's. *Photo courtesy of the Davenport Fire Museum.*

stepped out of bed and hurried over to the west window of her room. She looked out the window, and a man yelling up at her caught her eye. "The building is on fire!" he warned as he saw her silhouette in the window.

O'Toole, without time to process this tragic information, ran away from her window straight to her door and threw it open. Smoke billowed into her room, filling any clear air with its dark plumes. O'Toole would later report, "I opened my door and looked out into the hall. I smelled smoke and heard more screams on [the] floors below me. I didn't know how long the fire had been burning and I was afraid I would be trapped. Windows are barred and, anyway, I didn't relish the prospect of jumping from the third floor." She turned back toward her bed, grabbed her coat and shoes and returned to the hallway. Once there, she shouted back down the hall, warning residents of the fire. Mary Neighbors, an eighty-year-old longtime patient of the facility, emerged from around the corner. O'Toole didn't see anyone else coming, so together, they ran down the stairs to the center of the building. As they descended, the smoke got thicker and thicker, and they began to hear the loud crackling of the flames on the main floor. At the bottom of the stairs, they arrived in the central corridor, right next to Elnora's room, where the fire had started. In the corridor, O'Toole could hear the flames roaring behind the door that led to the front of the building and could see the embers' glow behind the frosted glass. This was a door she had entered and exited through hundreds of times. She knew that even if she could navigate the flames, the door was locked; it always was after nine o'clock.

O'Toole and Neighbors returned to the stairs and descended toward the basement, where the smoke was much thinner. O'Toole ushered Neighbors through the basement and out of the building, exiting on the south side into the bitter January air. From this side of the building, they had a straight line of sight to the main hospital and made their way over to the building through a swarm of newly arriving first responders. Once they made it to the main hospital, O'Toole finally looked back at St. Elizabeth's. She could see the building ablaze, with flames appearing out of windows on the east side. O'Toole had just escaped her workplace and her residence with only her shoes and the clothes on her back. She may not have realized it then, but she would never set foot in that building again.

The conditions of the building and the location of Elnora's room played a vital role in the fire's ability to spread. Within seconds after starting the blaze, Elnora exited her room through its only door, in the wall opposite the burning curtains. Fire needs three things to burn and keep burning: a heat source, fuel and oxygen. The heat source was supplied by the lighter Elnora used, which ignited the fire initially. As the fire spread across the fabric curtain, varnished wood and combustible walls and furniture, it constantly found fresh sources of fuel. As it engulfed the room and entered the hallway, every inch of the fire was met with new sources of wood and combustibles that encouraged it to spread and burn. As the fire moved into the hallway, up and down the dumbwaiter shaft and into the stairwell, it was fanned further by fresh sources of oxygen. All three components necessary to start and build a raging fire were present. On the contrary, nothing was present to halt or contain the blaze. No flame-retardant materials like at the main hospital to limit fuel, no sprinkler systems to reduce the heat, no closed stairwells or shafts to limit oxygen.

The upper floors of St. Elizabeth's housed a number of patients who were receiving treatment for non-mental-health-related illnesses, including some male patients. Nineteen-year-old Moline, Illinois native James "Jimmy" Stablein was one of these few male patients receiving care at St. Elizabeth's that night. He awoke from his bed on the third floor shortly after two

Josephine O'Toole, the only employee to escape safely from the fire, sits in Mercy Hospital on Saturday morning, still dressed in the coat she put on as she exited the burning building. *Photo courtesy of the Davenport Public Library.*

o'clock in the morning and noticed the subtle smell of smoke. Concerned, Jimmy rushed over to the bed of his fifty-five-year-old roommate, Bernard Anderson, and shook him awake. He then rushed to open the door and was pushed back by heat, smoke and flames, causing some minor burns.

Jimmy closed the door and, with his roommate, huddled by the iron-barred windows, waiting for rescue. Next door, they could hear a young kid shouting, "*Fire! Fire!* Get me out!" From down the hall, they could hear a woman screaming. It is believed that they barricaded themselves in their room for close to an hour before firemen (with Jimmy's help) were able to break through the bars and rescue Jimmy and his roommate from their worst nightmare. "When I finally got the bars pried open, I let my roommate go first," Jimmy stated. "He was so excited, he missed the ladder and fell almost twenty feet to the ground." Anderson sustained only some mild bruising from the fall.

Ellen Hildebrand was a nurse on the fourth floor of the adjacent Mercy hospital, in the obstetrics wing.

> *At about 2 o'clock I noticed a light flashing on the wall in the hallway. I thought it was an ambulance that pulled into St. Elizabeth's or St. John's. There was a light flashing. I went into the delivery room and looked out the window. It wasn't an ambulance, it was a fire shooting out of the window of the east side of the building of St. Elizabeth's, about half way down the building on the main floor.*

Once Ellen realized what she was looking at—orange embers blazing from an open first-floor window on the east side of the building—she immediately told hospital orderly Murray Francis.

Francis, looking north, confirmed the horrific sight and immediately ran down to the exit of the main building, across the lawn and to the front doors of the mental ward, which were now on fire. When he reached the doors, they were locked, so he broke the glass to get them open. Seeing the magnitude of the flames spreading quickly, Murray ran back to Mercy to tell the night supervisor, Francis Kelly, to call the fire department. Francis told Murray that this had already been done and that firemen were en route.

Kenneth Zepsy and two of his friends from Des Moines, Iowa, were at Mercy that night visiting his wife, who had traveled there to have an operation done at the hospital. The three of them were seated together in a waiting area, anticipating Mrs. Zepsy's release. Kenneth and his friends, Russell and Vern Carson, overheard the rumblings of a fire at the women's mental health facility, and they immediately ran outside toward St. Elizabeth's to see. When Russell Carson made it to the north side of the building, he could see women in the windows of the upper floors, behind metal bars, begging to get out. He then turned along the east side of the building and, looking up, could see flames coming from a window in the room previously occupied by Elnora. When he returned to the south side of the building, where an exit was, he spotted a short woman, whom he believed to weigh less than one hundred pounds, wearing a blue nightgown and a long robe, pacing back and forth. Witnesses would later corroborate that this was Elnora Epperly, the first occupant out of the building.

CHAPTER 6

THE FIRST ALARM

While the number of minutes that passed that night between the ignition of the fire and the first responders' arrival was relatively few, the fire spread quite quickly. The combination of highly combustible materials, open staircases, open flues and a cold, windy night led to the building acting as a matchbox. In addition, most patients were asleep and doors were closed, keeping many residents from becoming aware that the fire had spread before it was too late. The outdated construction and building design did not include fire-resistant materials within the walls, which allowed the fire to quickly penetrate the walls and spread from one room and one floor to another. Furthermore, the presence of open-air flues that allowed air to flow from one room to the next encouraged the flames to grow by supplying oxygen to the burning material. Disaster was imminent.

The first alarm call came in at 2:06 a.m.: "St. Elizabeth's Mental Ward in the rear of Mercy Hospital." This called for three engine companies, two ladder companies—one equipped with a sixty-five-foot ladder and the other with an eighty-five-foot ladder—and the chief's car. The chief's car on this call would be manned by second assistant fire chief Harry Lange. There were three men assigned to each apparatus except for the chief's car, which included the fire chief and his driver. The total number of men to respond to the first alarm was seventeen.

The first alarm call came into Engine Company No. 6 and the Central Fire Station. Located at 1410 Marquette Street, Engine Company No. 6 was just about ten blocks south of the fire. The firemen had retired to bed that

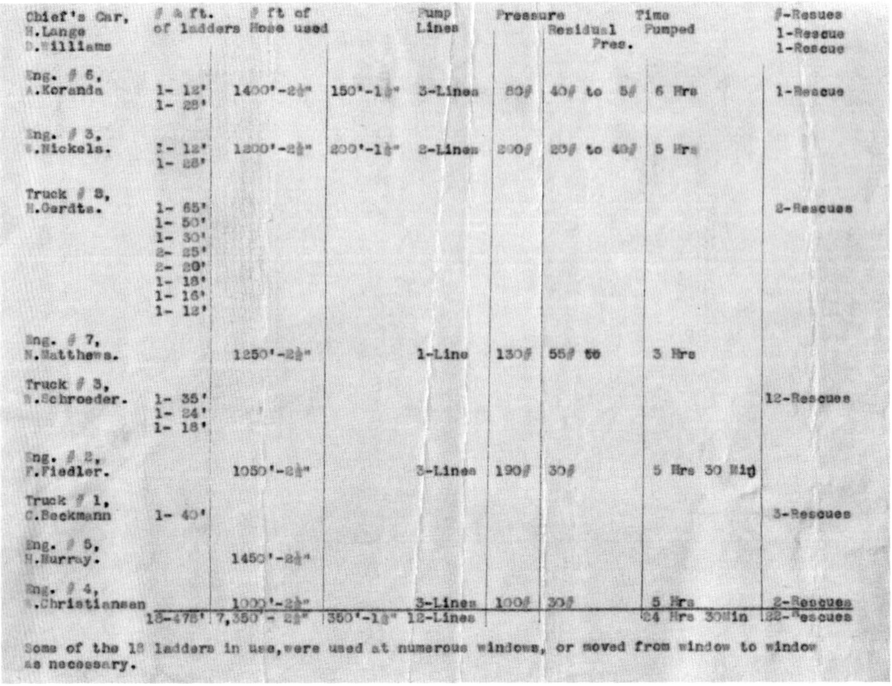

	# & ft. of ladders	# ft of Hose used		Pump Lines	Pressure	Residual Pres.	Time Pumped	#-Resues
Chief's Car, H.Lange D.Williams								 1-Rescue 1-Rescue
Eng. # 6, A.Koranda	1- 12' 1- 28'	1400'-2½"	150'-1½"	3-Lines	80#	40# to 5#	6 Hrs	1-Rescue
Eng. # 3, W.Nickels.	1- 12' 1- 28'	1200'-2½"	200'-1½"	2-Lines	200#	20# to 40#	5 Hrs	
Truck # 2, H.Gerdts.	1- 65' 1- 50' 1- 30' 2- 25' 2- 20' 1- 18' 1- 16' 1- 12'							2-Rescues
Eng. # 7, N.Matthews.		1250'-2½"		1-Line	130#	55# 50	3 Hrs	
Truck # 3, W.Schroeder.	1- 35' 1- 24' 1- 18'							12-Rescues
Eng. # 2, F.Fiedler.		1050'-2½"		3-Lines	190#	30#	5 Hrs 30 Min	
Truck # 1, C.Beckmann	1- 40'							3-Rescues
Eng. # 5, H.Murray.		1450'-2½"						
Eng. # 4, W.Christiansen		1000'-2½"		3-Lines	100#	30#	5 Hrs	2-Rescues
	18-478'	7,350' - 2½"	350'-1½"	12-Lines			24 Hrs 30Min	22-Rescues

Some of the 18 ladders in use, were used at numerous windows, or moved from window to window as necessary.

Fire department records detail the engines and trucks that arrived on the scene along with who was credited for rescues. *Photo courtesy of the Davenport Fire Museum.*

early morning when they were woken up by the siren of the first alarm call. They rushed to their truck, with fireman Phillip Axelrod in the driver's seat, Lieutenant Koranda sitting in the passenger seat and Pipeman Robert "Buzz" Sternberg seated behind them. The station doors were raised, and the engines went screeching out onto the road. The apparatus raced north, zooming up the gradual incline of Marquette, reaching speeds close to fifty miles per hour as their sirens echoed through rows of residential houses. The red and blue lights broke through the darkness of an otherwise quiet neighborhood where most were fast asleep, unaware of what was going on in their community. Engine Company No. 6 arrived at the hospital within two minutes of the alarm call, an elite response time, but the fire would prove to be an enemy that was too difficult to defeat even for these prompt and experienced firemen.

Engine Company No. 6 entered the driveway of the facility from the east side of the campus, off of Marquette Street. As they pulled up to the building, they could see two Sisters dressed in black and white standing at the north end of the building and one Sister looking on from the southwest corner, closer to them. As the engine pulled up to the fiery scene from Marquette

Street, looking toward the east side of the building, flames were already visibly protruding from three separate second-floor windows, some of them reaching the roof. The fire was fanned by a gusty southwest winter wind and was spreading quickly. "[The building] burned like paper," Lieutenant Koranda would later report.

Koranda noticed flames spilling out of the fire escape located on the second floor; this was the only fire escape in the whole building and happened to be located next to Elnora's room. Obviously, this would severely impede any rescue efforts that hadn't already taken place inside the building. The fire had been burning for no more than a few minutes, and it had already trapped a majority of the occupants of St. Elizabeth's inside. The strategy for rescue attempts seemed limited and the outcome of the blaze grim from the very moment of the firemen's arrival.

"In all my years on the fire department, I have never seen anything like it. It was plain hell," Lieutenant Koranda later reported. The first company to arrive had one objective: get as many people out of the building as possible.

Philip Axelrod, the Engine 6 chauffeur, brought the apparatus of Engine 6 to a stop just east of the building. The engine chauffeur was responsible for driving the truck and securing water into the fire hose on arrival. As Lieutenant Koranda and his men began exiting their rig near an available fire hydrant, they understood that their typical priority, firefighting, would be secondary on this frigid winter night. At this point, the building was looking like a total loss. Lieutenant Koranda immediately attempted to connect the fire hose but was interrupted by a scream of desperation that pierced the bitter cold. "Help me! Help me! I am going to burn to death!" came a voice from the southeast corner of the building. Lieutenant Koranda whipped his head around and saw a woman, small in stature, wearing a pink floral nightgown, prying at one side of a double window and trying to squeeze herself through the couple-inch gap she had created. Lieutenant Koranda immediately dropped the fire line and called his men to gather a ladder and hoist it up to that window.

Within a few moments, the ladder was in position, and the lieutenant scaled the rungs of the ladder to the desperate patient. The window at her location happened not to have any iron bars covering it. Now separated from her only by the window and a screen, he, too, tried to get the window to open, but it would not budge. He reached off balance and away from the ladder to the window next to it and got it to open halfway, and the woman left from in front of him and reappeared in the adjoining window. She began pushing the wire mesh screen outward. As she did so, Lieutenant

Firefighting efforts continue on the east side of the building, with water being sprayed into the room previously occupied by Marilyn Beals. *Photo courtesy of the Davenport Public Library.*

Koranda grabbed the screen and dropped it one story to the ground, and without permission or hesitation, the woman threw herself through the window frame and toward Lieutenant Koranda at the next window. The woman was now lying horizontal, supported by the restraining rail that spanned both windows.

Lieutenant Koranda grabbed the window frame and pinned the torso of the woman between him and the building, securing her momentarily. Her legs and feet remained on the windowsill of the window she had just attempted to exit. Lieutenant Koranda immediately called for another ladder to be put into position at the window she had exited. Meanwhile, the lieutenant shifted his feet and braced himself.

"Can you step over here to the ladder?" Lieutenant Koranda shouted at the woman. She nodded yes. He leaned out, away from the ladder, grabbing onto the restraining rail and supporting his weight with his hand on the window of the burning building. The woman turned around and crawled backward toward him, as he instructed her to do. Finally, he was able to secure her onto the top of the ladder, still facing toward the hell she narrowly escaped, and Koranda assisted her down the ladder, where she was met by hospital staff.

Neither Lieutenant Koranda nor the patient knew that this woman was one of very few people who would safely exit the burning building that night. Inside that building were over fifty more, all awaiting rescue.

Engine 6 chauffeur Phillip Axelrod had secured the water line to the hydrant and begun laying the line out in the direction of the basement of the building. Lieutenant Koranda joined him, and together, they entered the building for the first time. Once inside the basement, they saw the fire shooting down the dumbwaiter shaft—the shaft adjoined to Elnora's room. They noticed a downdraft of air and smoke forcing the fire into the west wall of the corridor in the basement.

Lieutenant Koranda, the first to arrive on the scene, later described how it only took "matter of minutes" for the fire to spread to most parts of the building. "It seemed like it went in every direction," he recalled.

Just a few moments behind Engine 6 were the firemen from Central Fire at the corner of Scott and Fourth Streets in Davenport's downtown. Second assistant fire chief Harry Lange and his chauffeur, Lieutenant Dwight Williams, pulled their car onto Scott Street heading west before turning north up Marquette Street. When Lange first heard that the call involved St. Elizabeth's, he immediately realized the possibility of loss of life that stood before the men working that night. As the chief's car raced north on Marquette Street, Lange and his driver volleyed comments back and forth about what might lie ahead of them. As they passed the station Engine Company No. 6, where Lieutenant Koranda had just departed from, Lange commented to his driver that he hoped it wouldn't be too involved when they got there. Moments later, as they crossed the intersection of Lombard and Marquette Streets, the inflamed St. Elizabeth's came into view. With his hands on the steering wheel, Lieutenant Williams leaned forward in his seat, nearly pressing his face to the windshield. The flames coming from the roof of the institution reflected off his eyes. The lieutenant remarked in astonishment, "Look at that baby roll."

Their vehicle entered the driveway from the east of the building and came to rest nearest the lonesome fire escape. Looking toward the otherwise dark building, Lange could see the glowing light of pockets of fire coming from six windows on the east side of the building near the fire escape.

Lange exited his vehicle and began making his way toward the building. He had only gotten about twenty-five feet from his car when he yelled back to Lieutenant Williams to call for a "third alarm" through the radio in their car. Lieutenant Williams verified the order, asking, "A third alarm?" The assistant chief, feeling the weight of the gravity of the situation he was now presented with, shouted back, "Yes!" His call for the "third alarm" meant that three additional engine companies would be sent, as well as a one-hundred-foot aerial truck. It also meant that all off-duty firemen were to report to the scene immediately. This included Davenport fire chief Lester Schick.

At 2:06 a.m., police officers Louis Hocke and Ted Hoeper were working the night shift patrolling central Davenport in their vehicle when a call came across the radio: "Woman in distress yelling from her room at St. Elizabeth's Hospital." Officers Hocke and Hoeper immediately headed in that direction to attend to the call. They arrived just as Lieutenant Koranda's Engine 6 was arriving on scene. Officer Hoeper followed the fire truck up the drive past the nurses' convent and immediately could see flames that appeared to be halfway up the building. He spun the car around and returned his vehicle to the corner of Lombard and Marquette Streets, where he dropped off Officer Hocke to work traffic control at that intersection. Officer Hoeper then returned his squad car to the hospital, where he parked and attempted to keep gathering onlookers safely away from the fire.

Chief Lange climbed the steps of the front porch on the south end of the building, entering through the front door onto the main floor. He continued toward the center of the building, and about eighteen to twenty feet from it, he came to a locked door, the same door that O'Toole and Mary Neighbors tried to exit earlier. Once he reached the door, he could see a crack in the frosted glass and a glow behind it. This alerted him that there was fire on the other side of the door and the glass was likely cracking due to the extreme heat that was produced.

Louis Hocke, seen here in his police uniform, was one of the first officers to arrive at the scene that night. *Photo courtesy of Ancestry.*

Chief Lange retreated, retracing his steps to the front porch, where he peered off the side and saw that the door to the basement was open. He ran back down the stairs and reentered the building through the basement. The basement at St. Elizabeth's housed the building's kitchen and served as a storage space and a place to access the tunnel that connected to St. John's and the laundry facility. However, Chief Lange, like most who arrived, didn't know about the use of the basement, and he entered assuming there would be opportunities for rescuing patients. This would not be the case, as most patients were housed on the third and fourth floors, above where the fire had started.

Once Chief Lange entered the basement, looking toward the north end, he could see flames coming down the dumbwaiter shaft. Embers from the burning material were falling down the shaft and out into the hallway. He returned outside and ordered his men to take a water line to the basement and soak the flames and to attempt to rescue any patients who might be down there. The men of the Central Station followed orders and administered water to the basement area, proceeding into the building to attempt rescue. There were, however, no patients located on this floor to be rescued, as the only people to use the basement that night had exited through the tunnels.

One block south of the hospital, fireman Darrell Doss was asleep in his home at 2112 Marquette Street. He heard the first sirens of Lieutenant Koranda's Engine 6 as they passed his home around 2:08 a.m. As those sounds terminated, he heard another siren approaching his home from a distance. He sat up in bed as the sounds got louder and then whirred past his two-story home. When he heard the third fire truck approaching, Doss arose and went to his window, watching as the red-and-blue blur sped by. As the third company passed, Doss knew immediately that there was a fire at Mercy Hospital.

Doss pulled on his clothes and stepped out into the open January air, where the windchill hovered just above zero degrees. As he stepped off his porch and ran toward the street to look north, about three hundred yards away, he could see the orange glow in the cold winter sky of the terrible blaze that was beginning to engulf St. Elizabeth's psychiatric ward. He knew he would be needed and took off running in that direction.

Doss arrived on the scene at approximately 2:09 a.m. and ran directly toward the burning building. Dressed in casual clothes, he joined his fire company, Davenport Truck No. 3, and immediately began assisting firemen in setting up the light system. Within a minute, Doss found Captain Lester Schick, who informed him that he was calling a second alarm.

The second alarm call went out at 2:10 a.m. The fire was gaining ground. This call included three more engine companies and one more ladder truck. Doss was able to get a ride back to the fire station to get his gear, to be able to assist further. After heading downtown to Fire Station No. 3, when he returned with equipment and his uniform, he found fellow Truck No. 3 member Elmer Schroeder, who had arrived with the second alarm. Together,

Fireman Darrell Doss hands a patient who was removed from the third floor to assistant fire chief Jim Quinn while fireman Irving Dengler waits to render aid. *Photo courtesy of the Davenport Public Library.*

they were able to enter the building and bring out a patient who had been trapped inside. After handing off the patient to the staff, Doss and Schroeder entered the building again, this time heading to the third floor.

"We crossed the entrance way there, through the room, opened the door there, went through the hallway," Doss recalled. "Flames were coming down the hallway and we were going to bust in the door across the hallway, but we noticed the paint was blistered all off the door and it was too dangerous to do anything about it, so we just ran out. There wasn't much of a chance—anybody in there would have been dead anyway from the amount of flame and heat."

Regardless of the challenge, Doss would spend the next fifteen hours assisting in firefighting, patient rescue and body recovery.

Lieutenant H. Gerdts of Davenport Truck No. 3 arrived at the scene with the first alarm call. On entering the building, he went up a flight of stairs and found the doors to the third floor locked. He turned around and saw the night supervisor, Anna Neal, behind him with a set of keys. Lieutenant Gerdts used the keys to open the double doors in anticipation of a rescue attempt. Instead, he was met with the overwhelming sight of raging fire and blinding smoke. Like most firemen who had arrived and rushed into the building, Lieutenant Gerdts wasn't wearing a mask. He turned to his left and found another hallway, hopeful for another chance to rescue the forty-five patients who were on the third and fourth floors. Again, he was faced with overwhelming heat from the flames and had to return down the staircase.

At the bottom of the staircase, now on the second floor, he ran into Assistant Chief Lange, the person who was currently in charge. "It's impossible, Chief!" Gerdts yelled over the sound of crackling wood and rushing water. "We can't get in there; it's too hot!" he continued. Lange nodded, signaling that he was aware of the treacherous conditions of the upper floors. The clock was ticking, and the two men knew that time was not in their favor.

"Go back and get a mask and try again," Captain Lange ordered. Lieutenant Gerdts obeyed the command, returned to his truck to don a smoke mask and made another brave attempt to navigate the third floor. This time he was only able to make it "two steps" onto the third floor before being forced to evacuate due to the conditions. Determined to rescue the desperate victims, Lieutenant Gerdts ascended the stairs to the fourth floor, hoping for more manageable conditions, but was met with more raging fire and all-encompassing smoke. Gerdts returned outside, this time heading to the west end of the building, where he assisted with rescuing women from the third floor—from outside the burning building.

A short distance east of St. Elizabeth's stood the Nurses' Convent, where Catholic nurses and staff of Mercy Hospital who desired to live on the hospital's campus were housed. One of these employees was Eileen Cox, an instructor of medical and surgical nursing at Mercy School of Nursing. She also happened to be the school's director of student help. On this night, her job duties would be magnified beyond any other experience she had previously had on Mercy's campus.

Cox was asleep in her bed on the third floor of the Nurses' Convent when the sharp sounds of screams and breaking glass pierced the otherwise quiet building. While the building was close to St. Elizabeth's, Cox's room didn't have a window that faced west toward the psychiatric ward. She bolted across the hall to the bathroom, which had a frosted glass east-facing window, forced the window up and looked across the lawn to the window with flames emerging from it on the main floor. She could see the fire growing from the room adjacent to the fire escape. Cox ran back to her room across the hall, threw her coat on over her pajamas and ran down the stairs to the second floor. Once there, she picked up the phone and

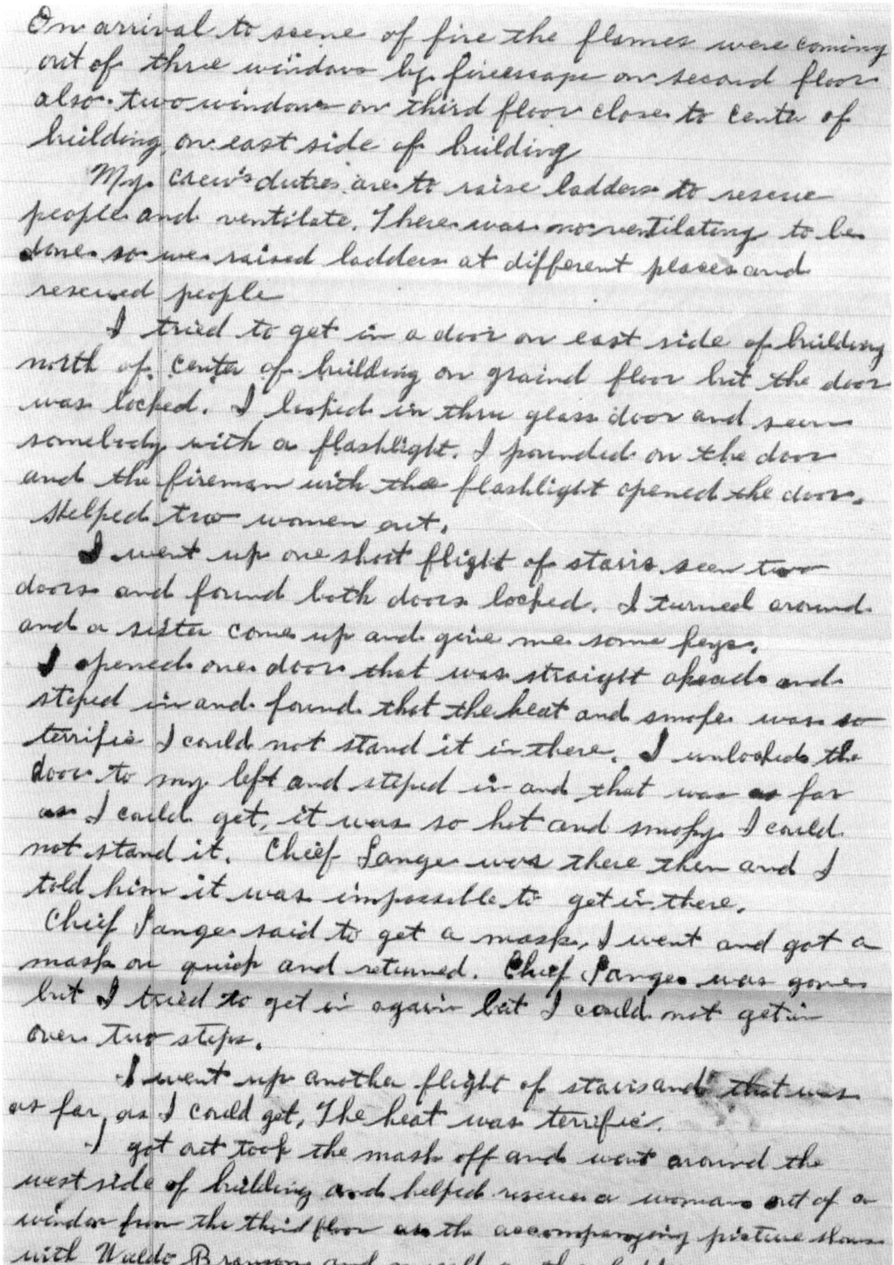

On arrival to scene of fire the flames were coming out of three windows by firescape on second floor also two windows on third floor close to center of building on east side of building

My crew's duties are to raise ladders to rescue people and ventilate. There was no ventilating to be done so we raised ladders at different places and rescued people

I tried to get in a door on east side of building north of center of building on ground floor but the door was locked. I looked in thru glass door and seen somebody with a flashlight. I pounded on the door and the fireman with the flashlight opened the door. Helped two women out.

I went up one short flight of stairs. seen two doors and found both doors locked. I turned around and a sister come up and give me some keys. I opened one door that was straight ahead and steped in and found that the heat and smoke was so terrific I could not stand it in there. I unlocked the door to my left and steped in and that was as far as I could get, it was so hot and smoky I could not stand it. Chief Lange was there then and I told him it was impossible to get in there.

Chief Lange said to get a mask. I went and got a mask on quick and returned. Chief Lange was gone but I tried to get in again but I could not get in over two steps.

I went up another flight of stairs and that was as far as I could get. The heat was terrific.

I got out took the mask off and went around the west side of building and helped rescue a woman out of a window from the third floor as the accompanying picture shows with Waldo Branson and myself on the ladder.

In page one of his handwritten account of the fire, Captain Harold Gerdts recalls some of the firefighting and rescue efforts he was involved in on that fateful night. *Photo courtesy of the Davenport Fire Museum.*

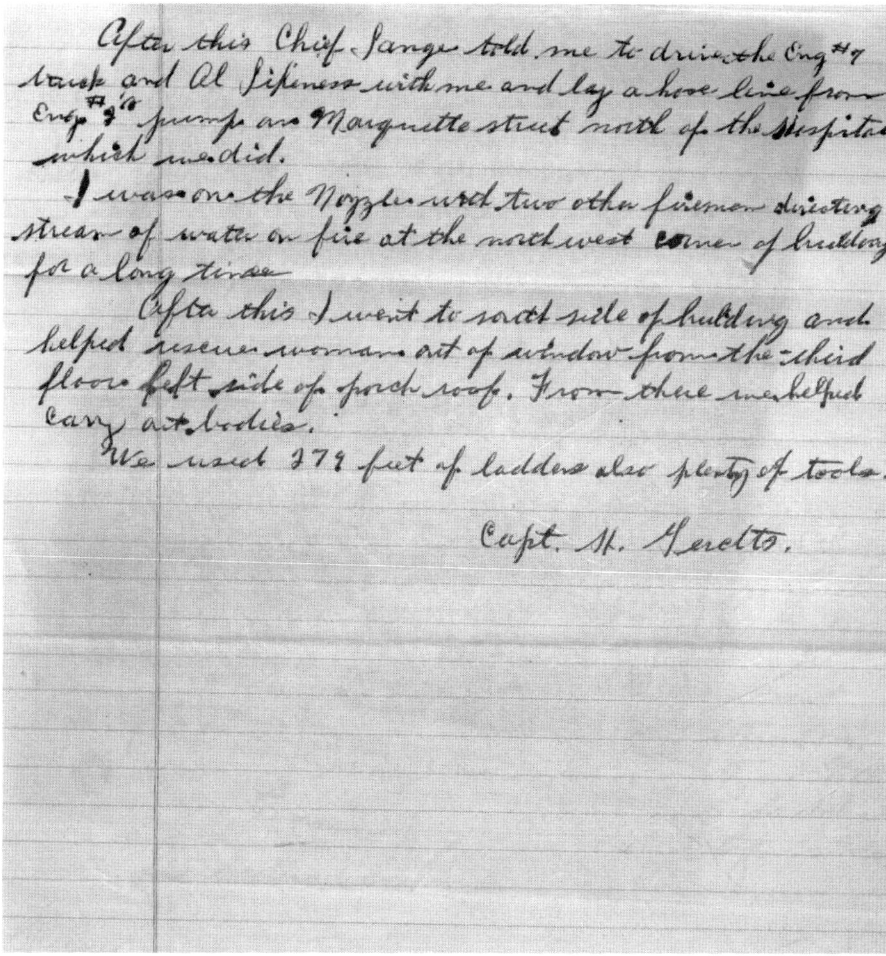

After this Chief Lange told me to drive the Eng #7 truck and Al Sifeness with me and lay a hose line from Eng #3's pump on Marquette street north of the Hospital which we did.

I was on the Nozzle with two other firemen directing stream of water on fire at the north west corner of building for a long time

After this I went to south side of building and helped rescue woman out of window from the third floor left side of porch roof. From there we helped carry out bodies.

We used 379 feet of ladders also plenty of tools.

Capt. H. Gerdts.

In page two of his handwritten account of the fire, Captain Harold Gerdts recalls the difficulties he had advancing into the building due to locked doors, smoke and fire. *Photo courtesy of the Davenport Fire Museum.*

dialed the number for Sister Mary Annetta, the director of student nurses. Moments later, she was standing on the lawn between the two buildings, grappling with the sight before her and determining how she could help. As she approached St. Elizabeth's, she saw nurses from the hospital bringing patients out of the building.

Cox, feeling the urge to help rescue these helpless women, ran up the steps of the porch on the south end of the building. At the top of the stairs, she was met by firemen, who encouraged her to return to the east side of the building. Here, she could help receive patients as they came off ladders after being pulled from the burning windows. Cox followed directions and returned to the east side of the building, where the smoke was billowing heavily out of every gap it could find. She observed two local firemen putting on their respirators, and she immediately grabbed a blanket and put it up to her face to protect her airway from the smoke. Cox then went up to these men and offered her help but was told that the fire was too heavy on the east side of the building and that rescue attempts were no longer possible.

At that point, Cox ran back along the south side of the building to the west side. When she arrived, she witnessed the most chilling sight she would ever behold. All along the three floors of the west side of the building, patients clung to the bars of their windows, begging for rescue. There were countless numbers of dark silhouettes backlit by the burning embers, pleading for help. They all looked down at her as their only hope of getting to safety. Cox scanned the west side of the building for ladders without success but remembered seeing a few of them on the south side of the building, near the porch. She also knew there were firemen over there.

This view shows the southwest corner of the building, where most of the rescue efforts were possible, due to that area having been impacted by fire the least. *Photo courtesy of the Davenport Public Library.*

Cox returned to the south side of the building, saw three firemen placing ladders and working on rescue and pleaded with them that ladders and men were needed on the west side of the building, where a number of patients anxiously awaited rescue. The response she received came as a surprise: "Go ahead and take one," one fireman responded. Nobody was excused from lending a hand.

Thirty-three-year-old nursing instructor Eileen Cox grabbed a ladder that was leaning against the brick facade and began dragging it toward the west side of St. Elizabeth's hospital. As she began placing the ladder, a helpful gloved hand assisted her, and she realized she had been followed by one of the three firemen. Together, they placed the ladder against the building, leaning toward a second-story window. The fireman scaled the ladder to the top, retrieving a patient and returning her safely to Cox on the ground. Together again, they moved the ladder to another window and rescued a second patient. Cox's efforts were heroic that night, and her intuition to move ladders and rescue from outside was directly responsible for saving some of the lives of those desperate women on the west side of the building.

Davenport Fire Department captain Lester Schick arrived at the scene around 2:20 a.m. On arrival, he quickly did a visual assessment of the scene. The north wall was engulfed in flames, and within minutes, the fire had spread up the two main stairwells and was bursting out of the iron-barred windows of the third floor. Schick quickly realized that the building was a total loss and this was now a defensive battle—get as many people out as possible, but do not attempt to save the structure. He also ordered power to the building be cut to try to limit any further catastrophe. At the same time, an emergency power unit was put into supply at the main hospital to ensure that, throughout the night, the main hospital would still have power to care for patients, including those it was receiving from the fire.

CHAPTER 7

SOAKED IN WATER

The fire chief for the Aluminum Company of America (ALCOA) was James J. Quinn, who lived at 2003 Marquette Street, two blocks south of St. Elizabeth's. He and his wife were asleep in their room when their young son came in, reporting he was hearing sirens. He was the son of a fire captain and, like most little boys, felt an adrenaline rush anytime the fire truck drove by the house. "There you go, Dad!" the young boy shouted into his parents' room. Quinn's wife ran to the front door and opened it just as Lieutenant Koranda's Engine Company No. 6 zoomed by. The fire chief knew the truck; he worked with those men regularly when not tending to ALCOA. He also knew that he needed to join them. Chief Quinn got dressed, ran out to his car and arrived at the scene a few minutes later.

Chief Quinn immediately found Davenport fire chief Lester Schick and assistant fire chief Harry Lange, both of whom had just arrived with the very engines that drove past his home a few minutes prior. "Do you need a little help, Les?" he inquired, somewhat jokingly. "I can sure use it," the chief responded. These three men—Lester Schick, Harry Lange and James Quinn—knew more about fire and rescue than any men in the Quad Cities, yet they, too, were somewhat helpless as this massive blaze began taking lives.

Chief Quinn decided he would assist in placing fire lines in areas that would best help to extinguish the fire. Schick, Koranda and Sternberg took a line down to the basement to work the fire that had reignited there and knocked it down again. After the line was placed and the men were administering the water, Schick returned to the outside of the building to assist in placing ladders up to the building for rescue.

Amy Rivera had been a patient of St. Elizabeth's for just under six months on the morning of the fire. Rivera had been committed to the hospital in July the previous year for what then was considered "manic-depression," better known today as bipolar disorder. She was categorized by her doctor as "manic type," suggesting that she experienced more mood swings that led to emotional highs than those that caused emotional lows and depression. While it is understood today that bipolar disorder is a lifelong condition, Rivera was sent to St. Elizabeth's with the idea that she would fully recover from her illness after receiving treatment.

Rivera's room was located on the main floor on the west side of the building, opposite where the fire started. The sound of screaming woke her up in the early morning hours, and once awake, she could hear crackling noises that sounded like wood burning in a fireplace. She also began to smell smoke. Rivera ran to her door and opened it, looking toward the centrally located reception room, where she was met with a sheet of flames engulfing the room and hallway. Once her door was open, the draft swept the smoke and flames toward her, forcing her to retreat to her room and shut the door. She ran across her room to the iron-barred windows and screamed until her voice became hoarse.

Since Rivera's room was on the west side of the building—the side opposite Marquette Street, where firemen began arriving—she was not immediately attended to. Eventually, firemen with a bar cutter arrived at her window and painstakingly removed the iron bars and Rivera.

Roy Porter of Davenport was a member of the volunteer unit called the Second Alarmers. He lived just seven blocks from the psychiatric facility. By profession, Porter ran a business putting up radio towers, but on this night, he would have a different job. The Second Alarmers was a volunteer unit that only operated alongside the local fire units when big fires broke out. It was first put together in 1947 by Davenport captain Lester Schick, with the help of his friend Ken Olson. The fire department was stretched thin after having a number of its members go off to war and never return to the job. The men trained at the Central Fire Department once every month, learning the skills and techniques used to assist when there was a big blaze. Thankfully, for those few years between 1947 and 1950, there hadn't been a fire large enough to call them into action—until the early morning hours of January 7, 1950.

Porter was lying in bed at 502 West Garfield when the phone rang during the darkest hours of the early morning.

"Hello?" Porter said into the telephone, his voice a little gravelly in the early morning hours. He didn't immediately know what time it was, but knew it was much too late for someone to be calling—it had to be important.

"Roy, this is Kenny," the answer sounded back to him. Porter knew the second he heard his friend Ken Olsen's voice that there was a fire somewhere and that it was a big one. He was right.

"Roy, Mercy Hospital is going up!" Olson reported. Ken grew up around the fire service, his dad having spent his entire career as a fireman. Certainly, he couldn't have imagined he would be summoning firemen to fight the deadliest fire in the history of the city.

Once he was alerted of the fire, Porter was out of his front door in mere moments. He pulled the door shut behind him with force, his feet barely touching the ground as he ran down the three steps of his front patio. Porter grew up hanging around the fire station; he was close friends with many of the men, including Captain Schick; and more than anything, he wanted to serve his community in this dire time of need.

Porter pulled out onto west Central Park Avenue, ignoring any suggestion of speed limits that night. It didn't matter much, anyway; nobody else was on those dirt roads at two o'clock in the morning. As he neared the corner of Marquette, coming from the northeast, he could begin to see the haze caused by the smoke and the southwest wind. Porter turned south onto Marquette and parked his car in the ditch, close to the scene but out of the way of other first responder vehicles. He hopped out of the car and went to his trunk to don his metal fire hat and raincoat—safety provisions weren't much for the volunteer squad.

Porter ran around the front to the west side of the building, where he quickly found a familiar face. Porter ran in his direction, and once he was within shouting distance, Schick yelled toward him, "I need you to go in with me." There were reports coming from the firemen that the inside was impassable, but Schick wanted to see for himself. He trusted Porter, a longtime friend, to go with him and assess the conditions inside.

Together, the fire captain and the volunteer firefighter ran up the stairs of the front porch and through the front door, into the terrible scene. Immediately, once inside of the vestibule, Schick and Porter heard a large roar grow louder and large bangs and cracking coming from above them. The floor above them was beginning to sag down toward them. Water seeped from the seams, and large pieces of building material had fallen onto

Bettendorf firemen spray water into the cupola on the fourth floor of the south side of the building, directly above the main entrance. *Photo courtesy of the Davenport Public Library.*

the varnished wooden floors. The captain analyzed the hallway from just inside the building and made it very clear to Porter what condition it was in. "The rest of that damn ceiling is comin' down. Let's get the f— out of here!" Schick ordered the two of them to retreat. As they turned and ran back out of the building, the third floor began collapsing. The two were mere seconds from being counted among the dead.

Once back outside, Porter looked up and saw a woman near a window trying to get out. "She was at the window trying to push the bars away. And they were desperately trying to chop away the wood frame of the windows. For just a moment I saw her face," Porter said. "That look of fear. Her screams. And then there was that whooshing sound and she was gone. The fire took her. For two or three months after, that's what I saw, the image of that woman."

A "Davenport Police Supplementary Report" describes what the scene looked like to police officers that morning:

> *Davenport Police Supplementary Report*
>
> *Date: 1-7-1950*
> *Time: 2:10 a.m.*
> *Offenses: Fire at Mercy Hospital*
>
> *Complaint: "We received a radio call that there was a bad fire at the St. Elizabeth's Home. When we arrived the building was a mass of fire. We pitched in and attempted to help the firemen as there was plenty of things to be done due to the building being so large and the fire was out of hand. Larry and I placed the ladders and other things that needed attention after the fire was under control. We assisted in handling the dead bodies as they were brought out of the building."—Officers Fee & Frauen*

As the rescue efforts continued, Davenport police patrolman Richard Fee, who was on duty that night, arrived at the scene and immediately jumped into action. "Flames were shooting out of the windows on the second and third floors, and I could see more fire on the roof of the building," Fee recalled. A ladder was drawn to a third-floor window, and Fee joined the charge, grabbing an axe and scaling the ladder to reach the third floor. Once he reached the iron-barred window, he began hacking with his axe at the anchor bolts that secured the iron to the window frame. The fire department did have keys to the windows at St. Elizabeth's, but what seemed like a fail-safe solution did not work that night. With the frigid temperatures and flames coming from the windows, locks failed, and keys oftentimes didn't work—breaking through the windows became more efficient.

As Patrolman Fee hacked for what seemed like twenty minutes, he could hear screams coming from other areas of the facility and could feel the sense of urgency building. Just as he was considering surrendering and finding another route, the anchor bolts gave way and the iron housing fell three stories to the frozen ground. Fee, dressed only in his police uniform and jacket, shouted back at the firemen to drench him with water from the hose lines. This would help prevent the fabric of his clothes from catching fire when in close contact with aggressive flames.

After being soaked in water, Fee disappeared into the smoke and fire of that third-floor room and saw a sight he promised to never forget. "When I entered the room, I found a group huddled together in silent bewilderment, apparently waiting for the fire to overtake them. The flames were all around them. They acted like creatures who had something new happening to them and didn't know just what to do about it."

Fee and fellow policeman Larry Frauen carried and escorted these women out. As flames began overtaking the room and searing their uniforms and skin, these officers rescued half a dozen patients, and other firemen brought them down to safety as Fee and Frauen returned into the structure.

Just a few minutes after receiving a phone call from his relative, local physician John Sunderbruch weaved past bystanders and cars as he approached on Marquette Street and arrived on the west side of the Mercy campus. As he drew closer, it became difficult to safely steer his vehicle between the buildings and find a place to park and get out. The thick, black smoke had grown so heavy that firemen were being pushed away from the east side of the building. The smoke had become so incredibly thick that as the doctor looked toward the east side of the building, he was unable to see any flames, as they had all been blanketed by the smoke.

Eventually, Dr. Sunderbruch stopped his car just southeast of the Nurses' Convent, less than fifty yards from the operating room of the hospital, where he had spent a great deal of time performing surgeries and other lifesaving procedures. The only lifesaving he would perform that night would not involve surgical skill or steady hands but rather evacuating patients from a burning building, something no medical degree could have prepared him for.

Dr. Sunderbruch ran north and west, past the Nurses' Convent and the cemetery, traversing through an enormous amount of people who had gathered for different purposes. As he got close to the east side of the building where the fire was raging the worst, he ran into a three firemen, introduced himself and said that he was there to serve in whatever way they needed him to. He turned around and recognized a familiar face, Officer Richard Fee.

"Dick, what can I do?" Sunderbruch asked.

"I need an axe gentlemen," Fee shot back at the three firemen.

The firemen supplied the axe that Officer Fee would soon use to rescue the aforementioned patients on the west side of the burning building. Holding the ladder that awful night as Officer Fee came up and down with rescued patients was none other than Dr. Sunderbruch, always eager to lend a hand.

Other police officers joined the scene to help rope off the area from spectators. A one-mile perimeter was also set up around the scene by police officers to ensure that no patients escaped the area. Blankets, when available, were tossed over patients as they exited the building, but due to the frigid temperatures and gusty winds, Fee described patients as "going from one hell to the next."

A "Davenport Police Supplementary Report" by Officer Hoeper describes what the scene looked like to police officers that morning:

> *Davenport Police Supplementary Report*
>
> *Date: 1-7-1950*
> *Time: 6:35 a.m.*
> *Offenses: Fire at St. Elizabeth's*
>
> *Complaint: "At app 2:06 AM we received a call to go to St. Elizabeth's,* [for] *a fire. When we got there we saw that there were flames coming out of the east side of the bldg, for some time after we got there* [there was] *one of us at Lombard and Marquette, this was Hocke, at that time I was at the roadway at the rear of Mercy keeping people out of the grounds. Sometime later one of the firemen asked me if I would come over by the fire, and keep the people back who were sneaking in around the hospital. I went over there on the west side of the burning bldg and saw that the firemen were having a difficult time of getting water pressure. At that time I could see Dick Fee on one of the ladders breaking in the windows, and pulling out of the bars. As I was there one of the sisters came to me and asked if something could be done about getting some patients out of the 3rd floor as there were about 15 of them there. Some other man there helped me to put one of the ladders which were lying on the ground, up to the window of the 3rd floor, and I then got one of the picks off the fire rig, and went up and broke the one window. A fireman then came up the ladder and took over and I then went down to keep back the people who were crowding too near the place. This I did for the rest of the night on the west side of the bldg."*

CHAPTER 8

FILLED TO CAPACITY

Over at the main building of Mercy Hospital, a new patient was being assessed for a laceration that occurred while exiting St. Elizabeth's—her name was Elnora Epperly. "Did I cause a lot of trouble?" Elnora asked night nurse Kathlyn Petersen. Believing she was referring to her wound, Petersen brushed off the question. Dr. Nuefield was the attending physician in the emergency room and overheard the conversation. He thought little of it; there was a lot of chaos that night, and Elnora was probably just overwhelmed. He continued on and treated her wounds, later deciding to keep her overnight for observation. Dr. Nuefield recalled later that Elnora kept repeating, "Would somebody please call my husband?"

Marjorie J. Malley, a nurse at Mercy Hospital, then took Elnora down the hallway to room 313, placing her in restraints in bed 3. "She appeared to be somewhat dazed. She had a cut on her left thumb and an abrasion that had been dressed on her right ankle." Malley would later mention that even though Elnora was well behaved, Malley had been given orders to place her in restraints that night, so she followed orders. Such restraints, leather straps that secured the patient's hands and feet, were utilized to protect both patients and staff.

It was evident all around Elnora that tragedy had struck this small community, and she began to realize the catastrophic situation she had caused. Nurse Marjorie Mally recalls that as Elnora was being treated, she overheard her being asked, "How did you do it?" Elnora replied, "With a cigarette lighter—I hope nobody was hurt." Unfortunately, her wish wouldn't come true.

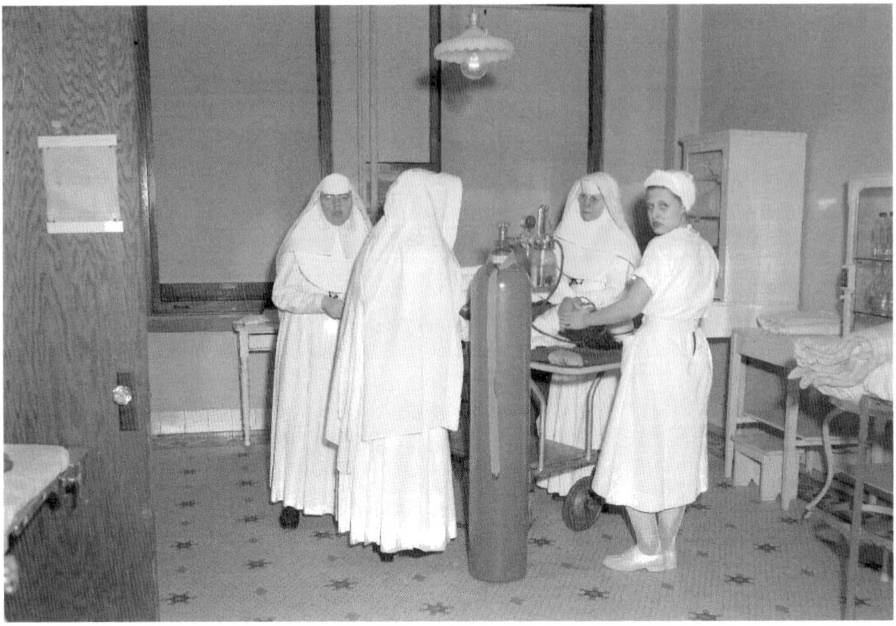

Sister Mary Gabriel, Sister Mary Aquinas and Sister Mary Julietta gather around a patient while care is being rendered by nurse Barbara Anderson. *Photo courtesy of the Davenport Public Library.*

Back inside St. Elizabeth's, the fire continued to grow and engulf the mostly wooden structure. Nurse's aides Willard Bennett and Gladys Oostendorf from nearby Mercy Hospital helped initiate some of the rescue efforts and assisted residents as they were leaving the building. They quickly began gathering and even carrying patients outside the main doors of the building to safety. On one occasion, Bennett argued with an elderly patient she was assisting because the woman insisted on returning to get her shoes. Later, as Bennett and Oostendorf reached the porch with two patients, they watched as an individual fell from a second-story window. The scene was unimaginable.[‡]

Once they reached the outside again, Bennett peered back at the west side of the building and could see her close friend, night supervisor Anna Neal, struggling alongside the flames while ushering out two patients from the second floor. At that time, Bennett saw a burst of flames that forced Neal back and watched as she fell to the ground, engulfed in fire and smoke.

‡ It is likely that this was Jimmy Stablein's roommate Bernard Anderson, who had fallen in a rush to get out of the building.

"I was very close to her," described Bennett. "Her daughter lived with me, and I helped raise her grandchildren. I guess that was the last time anyone saw her alive." Neal, who had only worked at the hospital for a matter of months, was the only employee to perish in the fire that night.

Once first assistant fire chief Walter Schroeder arrived, he began searching the building for patients who could be removed. "I had made a search of some of the rooms in the basement when I arrived on scene," Chief Schroeder recalled. "The second time I went into the building I found Mrs. Neal's body in a main floor room on the west side about ten feet past the partition." Chief Schroeder called for help and, with another fireman, carried Neal's charred body outside of the building to the staging area at Mercy Hospital where victims were being identified. Dr. Robert Nuefeld, the same physician who had treated Elnora Epperly for her laceration just moments before, officially pronounced Neal dead. She had suffered severe "burns on the face and chest" and died as a result of the burns and suffocation.

Sister Mary Gabriel, supervisor of St. Elizabeth's, arrived at the horrific scene with keys to the windows, which she immediately gave to the firemen.

A notice went out to all Mercy Hospital employees, doctors and nurses alike, to immediately report to the hospital and begin rendering aid. When they arrived, they were faced with a scene filled with terror. From the second- and third-floor windows, screams of desperation and physical agony could be heard. These female patients of St. Elizabeth's were there for ailments that were both mental and physical. Human instincts caused these women to pound at the iron-barred windows and scream for rescue.

Margaret Jane "Jennie" Woeber was the oldest patient at St. Elizabeth's, said to have lived there for over thirty years. As the fire burned on, the ninety-three-year-old Woeber was rescued from her room by firemen and transferred over to Mercy Hospital. While she was safely out of the fire, she was not out of the woods and would have to survive the destruction that the fire did to her physical condition. She would succumb to her injuries around five forty-five on Saturday evening.

Out of the seventeen fire companies from Davenport, fourteen of them had arrived at the scene that night to help fight the blaze. But that wasn't all: 10 volunteer firemen from the Green Acres Fire Department assisted, as did 10 more from the Bettendorf volunteer department. On top of that, a large number of Second Alarmers arrived to the scene, both to render aid and assist in rescuing patients as well as supply coffee, blankets and gloves to the firemen. All told, 107 firemen arrived at the scene that evening to offer assistance in this horrific event. At one point, fifteen fire hoses were counted to supply water to the fire. Eight different fire hydrants were available nearby, with only one not operating correctly due to a broken stem.

Outside of the building, Catholic Sisters in their black-and-white robes could be seen pacing the grounds, aiding victims and ushering survivors to the main hospital to receive treatment. Catholic chaplains arrived at the scene, administering their duties and offering the last rites of the Catholic Church to individuals who hadn't or might not survive (around 80 percent of the residents of St. Elizabeth's were Catholic).

Merchant policeman Bill Stegen was on shift to patrol downtown that night when he heard the second alarm call and reported to St. Elizabeth's. "I arrived about five minutes after the second alarm. The east side was aflame so I stepped around to the west and assisted a fireman with my flashlight while he attempted to cut through bars on the window," recalled Stegen. He remembered trying to cut through the bars with wire cutters, to no avail. He then assisted with an axe to chop at the windows, eventually getting through and aiding in the rescue efforts.

Minutes later, Stegan found himself back on the frozen ground, standing next to a Catholic Sister who was dressed in a white robe and had taken

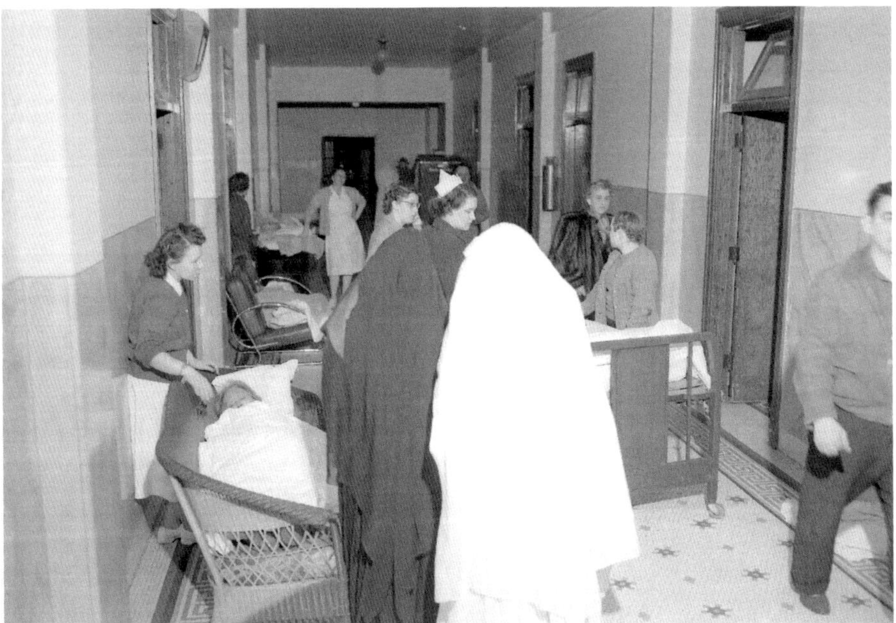

The halls of Mercy Hospital quickly became filled with staff and patients in the early morning hours of Saturday, January 7, 1950. *Photo courtesy of the Davenport Public Library.*

up the duty of distributing blankets to those who had been rescued. They stood together in silence, aghast at the scene that was playing out in front of them but unable to deliver meaningful aid. As this Sister and Stegan looked on, flames broke through the roof at the northwest corner of the building, providing visual evidence that fire had overtaken the fourth floor.

Neither Stegan nor the Sister broke their gaze as they looked on to the destruction. They didn't know each other and had never spoken in their life. Yet here they were, shoulder to shoulder, witnessing the most tragic event this community had ever seen. Still watching as the flames engulfed the roof of the fourth floor, Stegan asked the Sister, "Anybody on the upper floor?"

The Sister paused for a moment before answering, almost hoping that what she was about to say wouldn't be the truth. "It was filled to capacity," she responded soberly. There were nineteen patients housed on the fourth floor the night the fire broke out. Only two of them survived.

In the open air, the sound of breaking glass and screaming could be heard all across the campus. Firemen were heard shouting "Over here!" when they would discover new victims and "Send water!" after placing a fire hose. Ladders were shuffled along the side of the building, staying in place for minutes as firemen scaled them, only to be faced with the seemingly insurmountable task of breaking through the iron bars. Minutes would go by as firemen hacked at the windows, the desperate cries getting louder and louder and higher in pitch as death approached these trapped women.

One fact that needs to be understood in this most tragic event but might be difficult to imagine is the odor that was produced by the combustion of the materials in the building. This included wood, cloth and, unfortunately, tens of burned bodies. At different moments throughout the night, firemen and others who were anxiously engaged in rescuing patients and fighting the fire would have to pause and collect themselves, overcome by the horrific smell that was produced by the burned remains.

"It was the smell," remembered Second Alarmer Roy Porter, in an interview with the *Quad City Times* seventy years later. "You're just never prepared for the first time you smell that smell," he recalled as he mentally went back to that horrific night when he was only twenty-five years old.

On the ground, countless bystanders had begun arriving, being held back by Davenport policemen. Onlookers approached the building, some allowed the opportunity to assist in transporting victims across the lawn to the main hospital, others ushered away to a safe distance. All, however, wanted to see for themselves the flames and embers of the most tragic event the area had ever seen.

Millions of gallons of water were sprayed onto the fire, seeking to saturate what was an otherwise very combustible building. Around two thirty in the morning, after the fire had raged and destroyed the building for more than twenty minutes, loud bangs came from the north side of the building as the north end roof began collapsing. As the roof crashed into what remained of the wooden top floor, the third floor collapsed under the weight and fell onto the second floor. Now devoid of anything to support it, the north wall that had stood at that institution for seventy-eight years folded into the building. Bricks peeled away from the mortar one by one as they caromed toward the smoldering foundation below. As the weight fell on the wreckage, a cloud of debris, smoke and ash lifted into the air and a silence descended on the crowd of rescuers.

The glow of the fire began to subside, and the crowd on the lawn did, too. As enough firemen and water lines were deployed, the fire department was able to slowly coax the fire to an end at three forty-five in the morning, around ninety minutes after it had broken out. On the lawn, a Catholic chaplain could be seen; kneeling over a victim and placing his hands on the badly charred body, he initiated the last rites to the devout woman.

At 4:40 a.m., as the flames of the tragedy turned to embers, firemen were able to search the remaining sections of the building without fear of being overtaken by fire. While they did still have to worry about the building collapsing further or supporting structures failing, a number of firemen began the sickening objective of searching for and removing the bodies of the victims. After raising an aerial ladder to a third-floor window on the south side of the building, which still remained mostly intact, firemen discovered Mary Ruth Finnerty from Ottumwa, Iowa, who had "nearly drowned" from all the water that was put onto the structure. In a considerable amount of shock and in a serious condition, she was carried out of the building and taken to Mercy Hospital for further evaluation and treatment.

A local contractor who owned a fifty-foot boom-mounted clamshell offered his assistance in the early morning hours. With the assistance of the heavy machinery, the fire department, as well as a number of construction workers who had arrived at the scene, began the arduous process of turning over four floors of charred building material. Before the sun came up and less than three hours after the fire was started, the firemen had recovered thirty-seven bodies from the building and removed them to other places, including the hospital and six funeral homes. The next day, rescuers were told that there were two additional missing persons and the remains were to be scavenged again—two more bodies were found.

An aerial shot by a *Daily Times* photographer shows St. Elizabeth's after the fire, with Mercy Hospital to the left, St. John's above and the steam laundry facility to the right. *Photo courtesy of the Davenport Public Library.*

Scott County coroner C.H. Wildman had never before processed a scene like the one he would soon be charged to comb through. In fact, he had never really processed a scene of any magnitude before January 7, 1950. Wildman had been on the job for a total of six days when he was awoken at home and called to the Mercy Hospital campus. He had been elected by the Scott County Board of Supervisors on December 11, 1949, after a vacancy was created due to the resignation of the previous coroner, Roy McGinnis. McGinnis decided to resign from the position after asking for a salary raise and being told that the board had no ability to grant it.

To say that C.H. Wildman was prepared to face the events that January 7 held would be an overstatement. Prior to being selected as the county coroner, he owned Wildman Pharmacy in the Union Arcade building in downtown Davenport. Then, in the spring of 1949, Wildman sold his business to a competitor, Cooper's Pharmacy, and, according to the *Democrat and Leader*, was "not yet ready to announce his future plans." Those plans

The northwest corner of the remains of St. Elizabeth shows the northern wall missing after having collapsed during the fire. *Photo courtesy of the Davenport Public Library.*

apparently included working as the county coroner, alongside continuing to work as a pharmacist for the Schlegel Drug Company.

It had to have been a difficult start to his new career for the pharmacist-turned-coroner. Earlier that week, he managed the case of a twelve-year-old boy who was struck and killed in front of his home on Harrison Street while playing with his Christmas presents. Earlier that evening, around six o'clock, he attended a home on LeClaire Street in Davenport where a thirty-two-year-old army veteran ended his life with a .22-caliber rifle. After that, he returned to his home at 1507 Robeson Avenue in the adjoining town, Bettendorf, before being called out to the fire early that morning.

Soon after coroner Wildman arrived at the scene, he was joined by his medical examiner, Dr. Gordon Rock. As they walked up the grass east of the building, Wildman and Rock got their first glimpses of what they were in for. The sun was still out of view in the night sky, leaving the remaining darkness to help highlight pockets of glowing embers as the fire starved for combustible material. There was little left of St. Elizabeth's that wasn't charred, and the blackened fossil of the structure only gave clues as to what existed before the sun went down. The two watched as firemen carried out iron bed rails blackened from fire and smoldering remnants of mattresses. They knew they were in for a long few days ahead of them.

Wildman and Rock continued past the smoldering building and on toward the main hospital to begin assessing the human damage. When they arrived at Mercy, they were immediately faced with the sobering nature of the tragedy. The hallways were crammed with loved ones, some crying from having found their loved ones deceased, others frantic to discover where their loved ones might be and a few stunned as they tried to process what had taken place. As they passed through the halls, Wildman and Rock walked by gurneys covered in white sheets and rubber blankets that were often accompanied by a Catholic nun standing guard. They continued into the building and discovered a temporary morgue that had been set up on the first floor.

The temporary morgue had previously served as a classroom, with chairs and desks spread throughout the room. Now, those chairs and desks had been hastily rejected into the corners of the room and against the walls. The room had previously been a place that was typically full of life, optimism

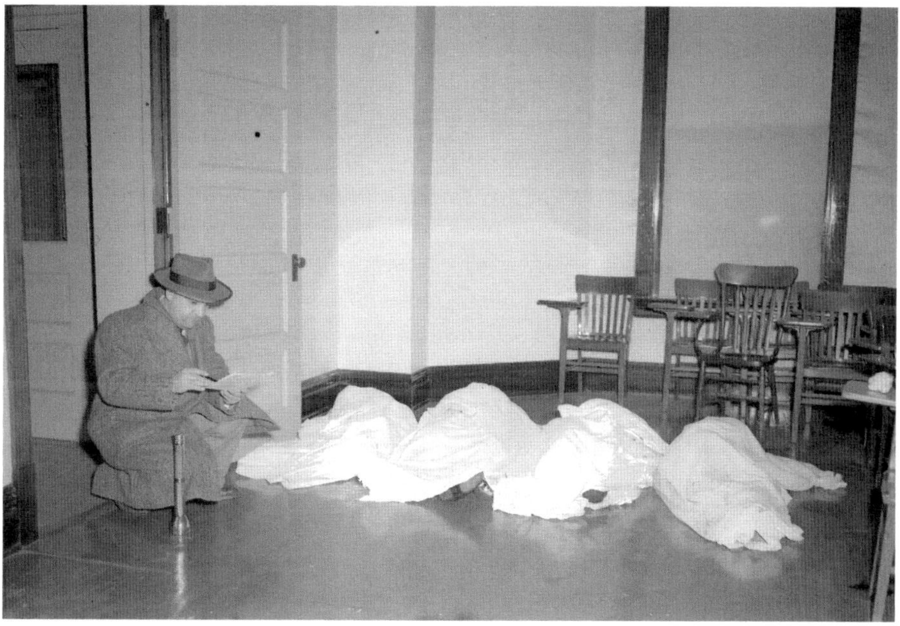

Coroner C.H. Wildman kneels with his flashlight and notebook while working to identify four victims who were placed in a temporary morgue—previously used as a nursing classroom—at Mercy Hospital. *Photo courtesy of the Davenport Public Library.*

and learning. Instead, today, it was being used to carry out the unimaginable task of tallying and identifying those who had lost their lives less than a few hours ago.

Inside the "morgue," a deafening silence hung in the room. So did the foul odor produced by the charred remains of those whose bodies lay there. Wildman scanned the room, attempting to make sense of the setting. On the tiled floor, covering a majority of the room, were white silhouettes, assembled in rows, resembling a bunch of white-clothed dominos thrown onto the floor. Scattered throughout the room were a few Catholic nuns, standing by to assist in identifying the bodies.

One item on the long list of difficulties that Wildman had to face was not knowing how many patients were in the hospital at the time of the fire. The information gathered among the staff indicated that there were about sixty patients total, plus two staff members. Wildman, at this point, was able to estimate that the casualty total was likely to reach upward of thirty deceased, meaning he hoped at least thirty had escaped. He would end up being wrong in his estimate.

As Wildman and the staff continued their work identifying patients, outside, a few hundred feet away, the foundation and remaining structure of St. Elizabeth's continued to smolder. White wisps of smoke danced away from the black ash and soot that covered the ground. As it rose, it was whisked away by the cold January wind. The ground crunched underfoot as firemen removed debris and continued searching for human forms. At 5:20 a.m., firemen discovered and removed two more bodies, bringing the total number of deceased up and of survivors down. These two bodies were so badly burned that they were unrecognizable. Forty minutes later, another series of bodies was discovered, adding insult to the unspeakable truth. All told, firemen removed twelve burned bodies from the building after the fire had subsided, bringing the total count of deceased to thirty-nine individuals. All of those twelve bodies that were removed from the building were found in the south section of the building, the area that so many had trouble escaping through due to multiple locked doors. This, of course, was also nearest to the area where the fire started—the southeast corner—meaning these flames burned the longest, were the hottest and were the most destructive.

As the sun began to rise in the eastern Iowa sky, the work of identifying individuals continued. Sister Mary Gabriel, who oversaw the institution; Sister Mary Winifred, who worked there as a nurse; and Sister Lucille Messick, who was a nurse's aide, assisted in the efforts. The first four bodies to be identified were those of nurse Anna Neal along with patients Maggie

Sisters Mary Winifred and Mary Garbriel meet with Coroner C.H. Wildman in a Davenport nursing home on Sunday, January 8, working to identify victims of the fire. *Photo courtesy of the Davenport Public Library.*

Tubberty, Minnie Madden and Mary Ryan. All four were removed from the south side of the building.

Moments later, with assistance from St. Elizabeth's psychiatric physician Dr. John Marker, officials were able to identify their fifth body. It ended up being the body of twenty-seven-year-old Marilyn Beals. Beals had become friends with Elnora Epperly, who initiated the fire, even though they both had stayed at St. Elizabeth's for only a short time. Epperly allegedly stopped by Beals's room on her way out of the facility when it was on fire, but for some unknown reason, Beals didn't follow her out. She was found in her room on the second or "main" floor, the room closest to where the fire had started. Her recovered body was so badly burned that it made physical recognition impossible. Instead, she was identified by her wedding ring, which was still on her finger. Her husband and two-year-old son were preparing for her to be released later that day, Saturday, January 7. Unfortunately, they never got the chance to see her again.

Four more bodies were tentatively identified around midday and into the afternoon on Saturday. The remains of fifty-four-year-old Marie Rauembuehler, thirty-eight-year-old Mary McNamara, eighty-three-year-old Rachel Dyar and eighty-five-year-old Alvina Kruse were all found together and positively identified by staff. It quickly became evident that the "temporary morgue" was not going to be capable of undergoing such a massive inquisition as to identify north of thirty victims. The decision was made by C.H. Wildman to call all six local funeral home and mortuary directors out to the scene to assist with postmortem care. This included the directors of Hill and Frederick, Everson and Anderson, Halligan, Runge, Horrigan and McGinnis.

As morticians began arriving, Wildman instructed them that bodies would have to be moved to their facilities to aid in the identifying and internment process. The main duty of the county coroner was to assist in the logistical and legal processes following a death in the county. With the death toll rising toward forty, that would be a tall order. Coroner Wildman also had to make one more instruction to the funeral homes that would have been relatively unique. He instructed each funeral director that the relatives of the individuals who would accept their loved ones' remains must sign a waiver. This waiver would include statements that the body had been "positively identified" by the person who signed it and they were accepting the body "unconditionally, waiving any right to disclaim the body at any future state."

As the clock struck 5:22 p.m. on Saturday afternoon, unbeknownst to those working on identification, another tally was added to the death toll—now rising up to forty women. Jane "Jennie" Woeber, the oldest patient at St. Elizabeth's, who was ninety-three years old, succumbed to her injuries and died at Mercy Hospital. Doctors said she had suffered from shock and smoke inhalation.

Family members who had arrived and were searching for their loved ones were now directed to one of the six funeral homes where that individual might be kept. Coroner Wildman and three other hospital staff members, including Sister Mary Winifred and Sister Mary Gabriel, the supervisor of the facility, traveled to these funeral homes in their continued efforts to identify and account for everyone. As they traveled and worked, using whatever context clues they could, they were able to whittle the list of the unidentified down to twenty-one by Sunday and eventually to sixteen by early in the week.

Oddly enough, on the deadliest day in the history of Mercy Hospital, the campus was also full of life. Inside Mercy, survivors from the incident were

Community officials gather in the ruins of the fire, attempting to find the cause of the blaze. *Left to right*: Reporter Paul Carson, attorney for Mercy Hospital Howard Kopf, fire chief Lester Schick, state fire marshals Charles Cornell and George Stebbins, Davenport fire marshal Othmar Mengels and William Blunk, the contractor who completed the most recent building updates at St. Elizabeth's. *Photo courtesy of the Davenport Public Library.*

being attended to, many of them receiving treatment for smoke inhalation and lacerations or burns from trying to escape. Fireman Lieutenant Al Koranda was treated by physicians for frostbite after having been soaked in water and continuing his lifesaving efforts. Koranda was the only rescue worker who had an injury from the fire.

Down on the first floor, tucked in between four windowless walls, sat the busiest person at Mercy that day, Bertha Blaine. "Mercy Hospital of Davenport, how can I direct your call?" she repeated time and time again into the receiver. Bertha was the switchboard operator who just happened to be scheduled to work the daylight hours of Saturday, January 7, 1950. The switchboard lit up like a Christmas tree as she triaged the never-ending stream of calls from people wanting information on the fire. Some wanted to know if what they heard was true; others wanted to know if their loved ones had been discovered. Sadly, Blaine had very few answers for those on the other end of the line.

An estimated fifty-five thousand people came to see the calamity as the sun came up on Saturday after the fire. This photo shows the line of cars on Marquette Street, looking south from the intersection with Lombard Street. *Photo courtesy of the Davenport Public Library.*

Above her on the second and third floors, a number of impromptu joyous reunions were held as family members shouted with euphoria at the sight of their loved one, still alive and well. Young Jimmy Stablein sat in the hallway of the third floor. He was still dressed in the pajama pants and slippers he wore to bed the night before. There was no real purpose for his presence at the hospital this many hours after the fire, except for simply that he needed

Evidence of the awful night before is still visible in the early morning hours of January 7, 1950, in this photo of the east side of the remains of the structure. *Photo courtesy of the Davenport Public Library.*

a ride. The nineteen-year-old had been rescued from the third floor after helping firemen chop at the iron bars on his window. He climbed down the ladder and was taken over to Mercy at about 3:15 a.m. He was released after it was determined that he had no injuries, but he remained there for more than twelve hours afterward. Finally, Jimmy's older sister Raye turned the corner of the west corridor of Mercy and made out the silhouette of her little brother, seated with his back against the wall and his knees to his chest in the hallway. Jimmy was a one-of-a-kind kid, and Raye would have easily been capable of picking him out of a crowd. Raye's slow, steady gait found more urgency, and she began running down the hall, arms open, toward her little brother. Behind her was Jimmy's twenty-five-year-old brother, Frank. While Jimmy was certainly happy to go home, he was also acutely aware of what he was leaving behind. "I lost my good radio, some of my Christmas presents, and all of my clothes," he would later tell a *Daily Times* reporter. Nevertheless, he knew he was one of the lucky ones, one of those in the minority. It was finally time for Jimmy to go home.

Downstairs in Mercy Hospital, staff continued providing treatment to Ruth Finnerty, who had been removed from the building in the early morning hours. Ruth, who was considered a "resident-employee" of St. Elizabeth's, finally succumbed to her injuries, bringing the final death toll up to forty-one.

Just to the north of Mercy Hospital, the soggy remnants of St. Elizabeth's began turning to ice. Areas where thousands of gallons of water had been pumped were now succumbing to the bitter Iowa cold. Forecasts called for temperatures to get down into the single digits and possibly below zero. Drops of water pulled downward by gravity slowly turned into icicles, growing larger and larger as time went on. Mattresses that had been soaked in water froze solid.

The work was mostly over but, in other ways, had just begun. The building that served as a staple to the community for over seventy years was now lifeless. No more staff, no more treatments, no more patients. All that was left was the smoldering foundation and the memories of a Davenport staple that had tragically burned to the ground.

CHAPTER 9

TICK TOCK

After staying in the hospital for the remainder of the day on Saturday, January 7, 1950, for losing a large amount of blood from her lacerations, Elnora Epperly was released on Sunday, January 8. Elnora and her husband, John, went to stay with her mother, Donna Carter, who lived at 926 Sixteenth Avenue in Moline, Illinois. "We didn't discuss the disaster at all because we didn't want to upset her," Carter recalled. "She insisted [on] having the radio on, though, and it wasn't long before she heard details [about the fire]."

As the week rolled on, Elnora started to become more curious and more and more agitated. At one point, she struck her mother while she was on the phone, accusing her of lying to the person on the other end of the receiver. Finally, she seemed to grow tired of her surroundings and announced on Wednesday to her husband and mother that she wanted to return to her home in Rock Island, to which John agreed, lacking much of a choice.

When the couple arrived at their home in Rock Island, Elnora seemed to get more and more upset about the circumstances surrounding the fire. She was holding a big secret inside and felt the persistent urge to let it go. No longer under the watchful eye of her mother, Elnora told John that she wanted to go to the authorities and tell them she had started the fire. At this point, John had no idea that his wife was anything more than just an innocent victim of the fire and lucky to escape with only a couple flesh wounds. He had no idea she was the person responsible for starting the blaze that led to the deaths of forty-one women.

John Epperly stands by Donna Carter, Elnora Epperly's mother, in her home after Elnora was taken to the Scott County Jail. Carter had been confined to a wheelchair since being in a car accident with her daughter. *Photo courtesy of the Davenport Public Library.*

Finally, after hours of persistence, John told Elnora that he would call the authorities and tell them what she had said. It was his belief that the authorities would understand she was mentally ill and would assure Elnora that she had nothing to do with starting the fire. Little did John know that he was terribly wrong in his assumptions and his phone call would be the beginning of a cascade of questions and interviews by authorities. In fact, his phone call would lead to his wife, who had just left the confinement of a monthlong stay in an institution, being back behind iron bars, confined and afraid, wondering if she had lost control of her life yet again.

Davenport Police Supplementary Report

Additional Information, Suspects, Details of Investigation, etc:

Date: 1-7-1950
Time: 7:45 a.m.
Offenses: Arson Re: Elnora Epperly

Complaint: Subject is 22 yrs old, married and resided at 2346 5½ Ave., Rock Island with her husband, John. John is employed by Poppelwell Motors, Rock Island. Records indicate that Elnora was admitted as a patient on 12-12-49 at the request of Dr. Hollander and her family. She was considered a private patient by the hospital authorities inasmuch as she was committed by her family. In the ward she was known as an average patient. She was discharged 1-8-50. She was under the supervision of Sister Mary Gabriel in the Ward at St. Elizabeth.

Officers Signature: Mielke Kruse

On Wednesday evening, January 11, 1950, Rock Island County investigator Harry Weinbrandt was at his home in Rock Island, Illinois, getting ready for bed when the phone rang. It was the Illinois state's attorney Bernard Moran, who had an assignment for Weinbrandt. He was told that Moran had received word that a Rock Island resident had some information about the fire that had taken place at the St. Elizabeth's hospital in nearby Davenport, Iowa. While the individual was willing to talk, the attorney's office wanted to secure an interview immediately. The individual's name was Elnora Epperly.

The Epperlys' home was a short distance from Harry Weinbrandt, less than five minutes away by car. The Epperlys lived in a small, five-hundred-square-foot ranch-style home near the end of a narrow dead-end street near downtown Rock Island. Weinbrandt parked his car on the street, walked up the few concrete steps and knocked on the door. John Epperly was there to greet him and welcomed him inside.

"Mr. and Mrs. Epperly, I am Detective Harry Weinbrandt with the Rock Island County Sheriff's Office. I understand that you have had something on your mind that you would like to discuss," said Weinbrandt, trying to delicately open a difficult conversation.

"Do you think I'm crazy?" Elnora blurted out from behind her husband.

"Well, no, Mrs. Epperly. I don't know you. I don't *think* so," replied the detective. He took a seat and settled in on the sofa in the Epperlys' living room.

"I'm the person that started the fire at St. Elizabeth's Hospital," confessed Elnora as she found a seat.

"Are you telling the truth?" replied Detective Weinbrandt.

"Yes."

Detective Weinbrandt continued asking her about the circumstances that led to the fire, including why she was there in the first place. "They tell me I'm nuts," said Elnora, "and they put me there."

The detective continued his questioning, asking why Elnora started the fire and how she was able to do it, considering all matches and cigarettes were supposed to have been removed from patients' rooms. Elnora recounted that after John left that evening, she began to be very nervous. She still had some cigarettes and John's lighter, so she smoked a few cigarettes and sat on the edge of her bed. After a while, she got up and began pacing around her room. She realized that she had been locked in and began wondering why that would be the case, as she had been told she was being released the next day.[§]

Tick tock. Tick tock. TICK tock.

The pendulum of the grandfather clock on the wall in their otherwise quiet living room grew louder and louder in Elnora's head.

TICK TOCK. TI—

"John, would you please shut that clock off?" she pleaded.

Elnora continued recalling her memory that she had become concerned her husband was "being killed" and in her mind, she *needed* to get out of that room to help him. At that point, she sat on the bed, lit the newspaper her husband had brought to her that evening, walked over to the window and lit the drapery. She knew by doing so she would cause commotion and a nurse would come open her door.

§ While Elnora was indeed set to be released on January 7, 1950, it was not because Dr. Hollander thought she had improved. On the contrary, he thought her lack of improvement warranted her being transferred to another facility, such as the one in Mount Pleasant, Iowa, that was used to caring for patients similar to Elnora.

Trying to understand the logic behind her mindset, the detective asked, "Well, did you see your husband that day?"

At that point, Detective Weinbrandt was able to get his first look into who Elnora Epperly was. As he finished the question, Elnora went "into a trance." Her eyes darted across the room from corner to corner, staring blankly at the walls of the small room at the front of their home. It was as if she was looking through the walls into another dimension of time and space. As Detective Weinbradt described it, "She kind of went into a coma." Elnora was leaving one state of mind and entering another, right in front of the detective. While it may have been hard to understand just why someone would set a room they were locked in on fire, Weinbrandt was beginning to get a glimpse of just how possible that was.

Detective Weinbrandt changed the subject to attempt to draw her back in.

"How old are you, Mrs. Epperly?" he redirected.

"Twenty-two," she responded as her eyes returned to the detective. He had her attention again. He asked her about her school days and where she graduated from. She talked about working for Royal Neighbors and McKesson Robbins Drug before leaving for a job at Walgreens. That was where she had bought the lighter as a Christmas present for John, with his initials, J.W.E., engraved on it. She had been working there for a while and bought it with her employee discount.

This Davenport Police evidence photograph shows the lighter used by Elnora Epperly to start the fire, with her husband's initials, J.W.E., inscribed. *Photo courtesy of the Davenport Fire Museum.*

Once Elnora was back in rhythm, she went back to describing the night of the fire. After she yelled from the room where the fire had just started, a nurse came to her door, opened it and she ran toward the center of the building. Elnora didn't know her by name but described that nurse as Anna Neal, the night supervisor and the only employee to die in the fire.

"After my door was opened, I had a good friend in a room a couple doors down from me, and I ran into the door of her room and hollered '*Fire!*' and I thought she followed me and I went out," she recalled, referring to Marilyn Beals. "I went through a room and came to a door that had glass and wire on it." She then described using a chair to break the glass and crawling through the opening, cutting her left hand and her right ankle on the way through.

Detective Weinbrandt looked at Elnora's left hand, where her thumb had been bandaged. He then looked down at her right ankle and saw the matching bandage there.

Elnora then described walking outside into the cold January air and roaming the grounds for a few moments. Soon, as others arrived outside of the building, she was ushered by a Catholic Sister over to the main hospital.

"I tried to tell them," Elnora pleaded, "but no one would pay any attention to what I was saying." She was getting more animated and was becoming somewhat emotional.

"Well, I'd like you to tell what you told me to the state's attorney. I know he will pay attention to what you are saying. Would you be willing to go down to his office with me tomorrow and tell him what you told me tonight?" asked Detective Weinbrandt.

The Epperlys agreed to meet at the state's attorney's office in Davenport at ten o'clock the next morning. Elnora was eager to do so and continued insisting, "I want you to believe that I did it because *I did*."

CHAPTER 10

CONFESSION

The next morning at the Scott County Attorney's Office, the Epperlys were nowhere to be found when ten o'clock rolled around. Had Elnora changed her mind? Did she think she would get in trouble telling her story to the state's attorney? Was John trying to protect her and keep her from going?

Detective Weinbrandt got back in his car and traveled across Centennial Bridge to the Epperlys' home, but nobody was there. He knew of Elnora's close relationship with her mother, Donna Carter, who had been crippled from the car accident, so he continued on to Carter's home in Moline, Illinois. Once there, he talked with Carter, who told him that John and Elnora had spent the night and just left.

Detective Weinbrandt returned to his car and traveled back to the Epperly home, where the Epperlys had just arrived, pulling their car up in front of their home. The detective jumped out and greeted them, telling them he had missed their presence at the attorney's office that morning. John replied that his wife was not feeling well the night before and they stayed up late at her mother's home. John apologized and agreed to ride back to Davenport with Detective Weinbrandt so Elnora could relay her story.

When they arrived at the Scott County Attorney's Office in downtown Davenport, they were introduced to the county attorney, Clark Filseth. John and Elnora sat down at a table across from Filseth. Court reporter David Hess was present in the room, along with Dr. John Marker. Detective Weinbrandt stayed out in the hallway; he had heard the story already.

"Well, Eldora—" opened Filseth.

"No, Elnora," she corrected. They were not off to a good start.

Filseth drew back a bit and sat up taller in his chair. In order to get the full confession he needed out of Elnora, he was going to have to be more careful with his words. Interviewing Elnora would be similar to a fencing match, with Filseth being tactful and on the defensive, carefully selecting specific times to make a move.

The attorney lobbed easy questions across the table to Elnora and began to paint a limited picture of her background. She was twenty-two years old and had been married to her husband, John, for three years. They hadn't yet conceived any children but wanted to. Elnora graduated from Rock Island Senior High School, across the river, when she was seventeen.

Filseth prepared for his first move.

"Now, Elnora, we've got you in here now to tell us—you talked to Mr. Harry Weinbrandt last night, didn't you, in Rock Island?"

"Yes," she replied.

"And we would like to question you further about what you told him and—"

"Well, can't you just take what I told him?" Elnora complained. It was obvious that Elnora was not fond of answering questions and certainly didn't enjoy recalling any of the details that led to the tragic events of January 7, 1950.

Clark Filseth, again going on the defensive, had to be cautious with what he said to the fragile Elnora. He explained that while he was aware she had spoken to Detective Weinbrandt in Illinois, he still needed her to explain to him the events that happened that night.

"Can't you just take what I told him?" she pleaded.

Filseth called Detective Weinbrandt back into the room. Weinbrandt had built a rapport with the Epperlys, something that Filseth, to this point, was severely lacking. He thought maybe with a familiar face's encouragement, Elnora might be more understanding that Filseth meant no harm. Weinbrandt stepped into the room and explained that while he did speak with her and take notes, he did not have her sign a sworn statement, and that is what they were in the Scott County Courthouse to do that morning.

Elnora grew impatient with the process and interrupted the two gentlemen: "I was scared, and I took John's cigarette lighter and lit the *Rock Island Argus* that he had brought over to me and set the drapes on fire that was in my room and opened the window, then went to the door and knocked on the door, which they had locked, and the nurse came, and I told her what I did."

Elnora Epperly, shielded by her husband, John, leaves the office of state's attorney Bernard Moran after confessing to starting the St. Elizabeth's fire. *Photo courtesy of the Davenport Public Library.*

While it certainly wasn't pretty, with that statement, Filseth got exactly what he needed out of Elnora.

"Was that at St. Elizabeth's?" Filseth asked.

"Yes, but I thought I was in Mercy Hospital. I didn't realize at the time when they took me that they was taking me to—" Elnora continued, before being interrupted by Dr. Marker.

"They did what?" Dr. Marker asked. Elnora was speaking very quickly and relatively quietly. Dr. Marker, who was seated farthest from her, wasn't able to keep up with her response.

Elnora never replied to Dr. Marker's question, but her medical history can fill in the gaps in what she was implying. Elnora's primary care physician was Dr. McCormick from neighboring Moline, Illinois. Dr. McCormick had received a call on Monday, December 12, 1949, from John Epperly, complaining to the physician that his wife was not well. John explained that ever since the auto accident Elnora was in with her mother when she was eighteen, she seemed to blame herself for everything and would become fixated on certain thoughts and ideas.

McCormick thought that Epperly would benefit from psychiatric care, so he enlisted the help of the psychiatrist Dr. Werner Hollander. That Monday afternoon, Dr. Hollander had just returned to town after being in Omaha, Nebraska, for the weekend. After listening to the message from Dr. McCormick on his answering machine, he drove over to Rock Island to Elnora's home. Once he assessed her in her home, he, with John's permission, took her to St. Elizabeth's to begin psychiatric care.

Back in the interview, Elnora seemed more comfortable with Dr. Marker, so he made his best attempt to move the questioning along. He asked her what was different about her condition on the night she decided to set the curtains on fire.

"You know," she responded, looking down and avoiding eye contact, "the way I figure on that, I don't think it's nobody's business but my own."

Dr. Marker reassured Elnora that indeed, it wasn't anybody else's business, but he just wanted to talk to her. He asked her why she felt the need to set anything on fire that night.

"Because I was scared!" she shouted toward the floor, avoiding eye contact with the physician. "I thought they had killed John." Her shoulders slouched, and she sank lower into the wooden-framed chair.

In an attempt to make her feel comfortable, Dr. Marker suggested, "I wish you'd come over here and sit by me and talk to me instead of—"

Elnora interrupted, eager to stop his sentence before he could finish, "Well, I don't think it's any of your business. My doctor is Dr. Hollander."

"Are you afraid of me?" Dr. Marker asked. He was speaking to her using the tone a pediatrician would use with a child.

"I don't trust doctors—all they want to do is cut you open and see what you're made of." Elnora's eyebrows furrowed and her forehead wrinkled as she finished her sentence. The words came out of her mouth as if she was too disgusted to let them stay in there.

Elnora explained that she had recently gone to two separate doctors who wanted to "cut her open." After having trouble conceiving a child and feeling some abdominal pain, Elnora went to Dr. Linden, an obstetrician, at the recommendation of a friend. Dr. Linden told her she had cysts on her ovaries and recommended doing an operation. After talking it over with her mother and husband, she decided to get a second opinion and sought the help of her mother's physician, Dr. deSilva. He agreed with her previous doctor's opinion and performed an operation on Elnora, removing her ovarian cysts. The Epperlys again attempted to conceive without success, so she returned to Dr. deSilva.

"I went to see him, and he told me my womb was infertile—that it hadn't growed since I was around thirteen and that was probably why [she struggled getting pregnant]."

"Did that give you quite a shock when he told you that?" asked Dr. Marker.

"Yes, it did. I supposed it meant another operation," replied Elnora. It became apparent that she had a real fear of medical procedures.

"Tell me why you thought someone might hurt John." Dr. Marker was trying to redirect Elnora's thoughts back to the night of the fire. She explained to him that ever since entering the facility for treatment, she felt like the staff didn't want her to see her husband, John. She said a doctor had told her that doing so might cause a relapse in her condition. This upset Elnora deeply, particularly when other residents were allowed to go home at Christmas, while she was left at the hospital. She recalled that on that night, she believed John had been killed and she needed to get out of the hospital because nobody else knew she was there.

"Did they use to give you some electric treatments, Elnora?" Dr. Marker asked.

"Yes," she responded timidly.

"And were they pretty severe on you?" Dr. Marker assumed.

"No," she replied.

"Didn't bother you a great deal?" the doctor pried further.

"No," she repeated, somewhat annoyed by the line of questioning.

Dr. Marker was acutely aware of the treatments administered at St. Elizabeth's, as he was one of the treating physicians at the hospital. Dr. Marker was responsible for three of the female patients at the hospital on the night of the fire, including Elnora's neighbor at the facility, Marilyn Beals. He knew the severity of the treatments that were received by patients whose conditions were as poor as Elnora's.

Dr. Marker continued questioning Elnora, trying to get to the bottom of why she felt the need to escape from the mental health facility and why exactly she believed John had been killed. The most common response that would be heard in the room that day was some version of "I don't think that is any of your business." On one occasion, Dr. Marker even tried to get an answer out of John—and Elnora quickly shut that down, threatening to divorce him if he responded.

"Were you locked in the room that night?" the doctor continued.

"Yes," Elnora replied. "It seems like any time they felt like it, they would lock me in my room, and, I mean, I hadn't done anything to be locked in my room, and I don't like the idea of being locked in a room with bars on the window. Well, who would?"

Elnora explained again that after she set fire to the curtains and called for help, she ran down the hallway, with the lighter still in her hand, toward the front door. At one point, she threw a chair at the glass window in a locked door, shattering it enough to allow her to crawl through it. She then tossed the lighter into a different room and ran out the front door, where she found someone she believed to be a nurse.

Scott County officials gather to discuss the legal course of action with Elnora Epperly. *Seated, left to right*: Assistant Scott County attorney Martin Leir, Detective Captain Harold Thordsen, Davenport fire marshal Othmar Mangels and Dr. John Marker. *Standing, left to right*: state deputy fire marshal Ed Stebbins, fire chief Lester Schick, Rock Island deputy sheriff Harry Weinbrandt, special investigator Walter Gage, Scott County attorney Clark Filseth and, behind Filseth, assistant county attorney Charles Rehling. *Photo courtesy of the Davenport Public Library.*

Filseth chimed in, "Elnora, do you think you did the right thing when you set fire to that curtain?" By this time in the questioning, Elnora had gone on a series of tangents that had nothing to do with the events that took place on January 7, 1950. It's possible that Filseth was growing tired of the conversation, eager to get what he needed. It's understandable why he would feel that way—there were forty-one deceased women, and he was responsible for bringing the individual who caused their death to justice. He wasn't willing to waste time, especially when he believed he had the culprit sitting across from him.

Filseth was back on the attack, ready to pierce the armor of his opponent.

"Now, you actually set fire to this curtain? You actually did that?" Filseth asked.

"Yes, I did. I told you that a million times," Elnora responded in agitation. Their less-than-ideal working relationship was evident again.

"It isn't something you're imagining, now?" prodded Filseth.

"No," volleyed Elnora.

"You really did it?" Filseth confirmed.

"I ought to know what I did," she replied bluntly.

"You know that you are telling this now to law enforcement officers?" Filseth continued. He was careful to ensure that her confession would be sturdy enough to stand up in court.

"Yes," she replied.

"Elnora, you tell us what you think they ought to do with you for setting fire to that?" Dr. Marker interjected.

"Well, I suppose they will lock me up and make me stand trial," she shrugged.

"For what?" asked Dr. Marker. He was trying to find out if Elnora really did understand the magnitude of what she had done.

"I suppose you'd call it murder, wouldn't you—mass murder? I'll probably end up in the electric chair." The chilling words rolled out of her mouth with a tone that didn't quite fit the sentence. While Elnora intellectually understood the gravity, she lacked the emotion you might expect of someone in her situation. This was likely due to the mental illness she had been undergoing treatment for—an illness that was surely worsened by the tragic circumstances she found herself entangled in.

"If you locked me up, I'd rather be dead!" Epperly shouted at Dr. Marker. At this point in the conversation, there was very little use for being friendly anymore. Filseth had received the confession he needed, and Dr. Marker was able to get to a depth with Elnora that they had yet to witness—raw emotion.

"Well, you were locked up out there," Dr. Marker reminded her, referring to Elnora's time spent behind the iron bars at St. Elizabeth.

"Yes, I was. How would you be if you was behind locked doors and couldn't go outdoors, only when they felt like taking you for a walk?" At that moment, whether he fully realized it or not, Dr. Marker had discovered two perhaps subconscious reasons Elnora Epperly lit the *Rock Island Argus* and held it up to the fabric curtains on that cold night in January—fear and lack of freedom.

Elnora Epperly had been confined to the seventy-year-old building for the better part of a month. She was young, only twenty-two years old, and should have been living some of the most carefree years of her life. Others her age were having children, making a living, keeping house, enjoying the outdoors, going for bike rides and soaking up the tender moments that make life worthwhile. Instead, in her eyes, she was imprisoned—locked away during the holidays, relegated to the four walls of her room and one iron-barred window. She was left with nothing but her own thoughts—thoughts that made her feel like the weight of the world was on her shoulders. She felt responsible for everything: the car accident that left her mother crippled, her unexplained infertility and the family's financial struggles. People didn't think Elnora Epperly was sick; they thought she was insane—the sign even said so on the door. Her life was slipping away from her, and all she had left was her loyal husband, which is why she needed so desperately to get to him. Holding his lighter with the initials J.W.E. in her hand had to make her miss his presence even more. So she succumbed to the thoughts of her mentally unstable mind and did the only thing within her power as a physical way out. Sadly, her actions would not result in freedom or reduced fear for long, especially when she was responsible for the deaths of forty-one innocent women.

CHAPTER 11

BACK BEHIND IRON BARS

With the confession in hand and the authorities pleased with the results, on Thursday, January 12, 1950, Elnora Epperly was taken to the women's ward of the Scott County Jail and detained in relation to a charge of the first-degree murder of Anna Neal. She was being held on no bond, consistent with the law in Iowa for someone charged with first-degree murder. John Epperly and Donna Carter could not believe what they were witnessing.

"How can they throw her into a jail cell?" John wept. "They know she is mentally ill! This is the worst thing that could happen! She belongs in a hospital."

The family immediately sought the legal services of attorney Charles B. Kaufmann, who promptly stated his belief that Elnora was innocent. "I am convinced that she did not set the fire in that hospital," Kaufmann told the *Daily Times*.

Scott County attorney Clark Filseth explained that because she had not previously been adjudicated as insane and she was a "voluntary patient" at St. Elizabeth's, the women's ward was the right place for her to be while the rest of the legal process played out. That process would include a preliminary hearing and the gathering of a jury for a sanity hearing. If Elnora entered ~~into~~ a plea of insanity, testimony would then be heard by the sanity commission and a determination would be made. If found insane at the time of the fire, Elnora would be confined to a ward in the Anamosa, Iowa reformatory.

On January 14, after visiting with his client at the Scott County Jail, attorney Kauffmann indicated that his client would be entering a plea of insanity if the case continued up through the district court and if she was considered sane by the sanity commission. Kaufmann was also able to get his client moved to the hospital ward of the jail to have better around-the-clock care.

As for whether Mercy Hospital would shoulder any of the blame for the tragic event, county attorney Filseth said, "There is no indication of negligence on the part of the hospital."

So there Epperly sat, the only patient in the hospital ward of the Scott County Jail and one of only two female inmates jail-wide. Epperly would stay inside the jail until the sanity hearing could take place, a meeting that was delayed on multiple occasions for various reasons. Her cell consisted of a typical hospital bed, a bench and a small table. She received visits from staff every two hours and was allowed to smoke when they were present; the staff member was the only one allowed to handle the lighter. Elnora sat and read magazines—no newspapers were allowed, even though she requested them—and received visits from her family and legal counsel only. Jail staff reported that she frequently ordered the "cold plate" for meals, which included lunch meat, cheese, baked pork and beans, toast, pickles and olives.

As far as her behavior was concerned, Elnora was a model citizen. "I wish all our women prisoners were as docile as she is," said Scott County sheriff Walter Beuse.

On Wednesday, January 18, at one thirty in the afternoon, Elnora was brought from her jail cell to the Scott County Courthouse on the third floor, where the sanity hearing finally commenced. The hearing was conducted by attorney Henry Jebens, physician Dr. W.S. Bindford and district court clerk Elmer Jens. Others in that meeting included Epperly's physician, Dr. Werner Hollander; physician Dr. John Marker; county attorney Clark Filseth; family-appointed attorney Charles B. Kaufmann; and Elnora's family. One of the family members present at the hearing was Elnora's father, John Marco, who had driven out from Washington state to support his daughter. The *Daily Times* reported that during the hearing, Elnora's physician, Dr. Werner Hollander, declared that the actions taken by Elnora to set the fire were the result of the effects of the shock treatment given to her while at the hospital.¶

The following morning, January 19, 1950, the clerk of the Scott County District Court announced that the commission had determined Elnora to be criminally insane and cited a diagnosis of "dementia praecox paranoid"

¶ Dr. Hollander's belief that Elnora started the fire as a result of the shock treatment can be backed up by some evidence. He had stated that she had been undergoing both types of shock treatment, insulin shock therapy and electric shock therapy. Historically, it had been reported that patients often felt restless and agitated following treatments, which certainly matched Elnora's demeanor on the night of the fire. Lastly, despite her mental illness, Elnora had never shown aggression or presented any danger prior to entering St. Elizabeth's. The only reason she was locked into her room was because, at that time of night, she was considered a bit of a nuisance.

caused by an automobile accident in 1946 and her "disappointment at sterility." Arrangements were made to transfer Elnora to the state mental health hospital in Mount Pleasant, Iowa, approximately ninety minutes southwest of Davenport. The state would then coordinate with her home state of Illinois to transfer her to one of its mental health hospitals.

On Friday, January 20, Elnora Epperly was transferred from the Scott County Jail to the state mental health hospital in Mount Pleasant by Deputy Sheriff Al Bloom. While Elnora was confined to that facility, a great amount of work was taking place outside of its walls.

Iowa governor William S. Beardsley granted a transfer of Elnora to the State of Illinois and Rock Island County, and she was soon transferred to an East Moline mental health facility.

Meanwhile, on Monday, January 30, eighty-year-old Christine Papenbrock passed away at Mercy Hospital in Davenport at 10:20 p.m. Papenbrock was rescued from the fire on January 7 and had been a resident of St. Elizabeth's for over ten years. She was a lifelong Davenport resident and supposedly had been battling an illness while in the hospital. While it is undetermined whether her illness was related to the fire she was rescued from just three and a half weeks prior, her death certificate recorded her cause of death as a "coronary occlusion."

On Thursday, February 2, the long-awaited coroner's inquest organized by C.H. Wildman began in the west courtroom of the Scott County Courthouse. Fourteen individuals testified to the jury that day, including policeman Richard Fee, assistant fire chief James Quinn, Davenport firemen Darrell Doss and Phillip Axelrod, fire lieutenant Alvin Koranda, Davenport fire marshal Othmar Mangels, second assistant fire chief Harry Lange and fire chief Lester Schick. During the inquest, a number of significant details were brought up that would later help the jury to come to a conclusion.

State fire marshal Charles Cornell cited a great deal of evidence suggesting the fire started in the room of Elnora Epperly. "Further proof that this was the point of origin is that on the outside walls just above the window, there was a considerable amount of black soot deposit, which would indicate that the black smoke and flame was coming out of this window before the fire had burned up through the room above and through the roof," Cornell explained. "This room has been identified as the one occupied by Mrs. Elnora Epperly." Later, Dr. John Sunderbruch testified that while treating patients at the hospital on the night of the fire, he overheard a patient admitting to setting fire to the building with a cigarette lighter.

Dr. Werner Hollander also took the stand to testify at the inquest hearing. He reported how he had urged the hospital not to lock Elnora in her room, yet she had been against his judgment. When he had first arrived at the hospital that night, he recalled seeing Elnora in the convent and being told by a nurse that Elnora had suggested she had started the fire. He said at the time he didn't think much of it, but later, she confessed the same thing to him.

Finally, pictures of broken glass from the door that Elnora allegedly broke through were presented to the jury. These details, combined with her confession, were enough for the jury to unanimously consider her guilty of first-degree murder and deem her to have been of unsound mind when she committed such a heinous act. It took them only fifty minutes of deliberation.

Elnora continued treatment in the East Moline state hospital, and in early March, Scott County attorney Clark Filseth announced that if no proof was found or witnesses came forward refuting the claim, he expected that the Scott County grand jury would return a bill of "no" when it met in April 1950. This would release Elnora of all criminal charges related to the fire, with the possibility of a grand jury bringing them against her at a later date if new evidence were to come forward.

Filseth was correct in his assumption. On April 27, 1950, the Scott County District Court grand jury issued a "no bill" and concluded that, indeed, Epperly was not of sound mind when she committed the acts that led to the death of at least forty-one individuals. This was consistent with the findings of the Scott County District Court's commission in January and the coroner's jury's findings in February.

In June 1950, after Elnora had spent four months in the East Moline facility, superintendent Dr. A.H. Wolff granted her "conditional discharge for one year." This released her to her husband under the order that if she needed further treatment, he would have to contact the appropriate authorities. The family attorney, Charles B. Kaufmann, reported that Elnora had improved both physically and mentally after having been released from the mental institution and that she could no longer recall the fire.

Six months later, on January 7, 1951, the minute hand on the clock ticked again, signaling 2:06 a.m., but there was little noise in the cold Iowa air. No screaming from patients who were engulfed in flames and thick, dark smoke. No whirring of sirens as firemen rushed toward the tragic scene. No water being poured, no hoses being laid, no ladders being braced against windowsills. There was no death, no destruction and no noise. Nuns from the local order of the Sisters of Mercy gingerly walked the ground where

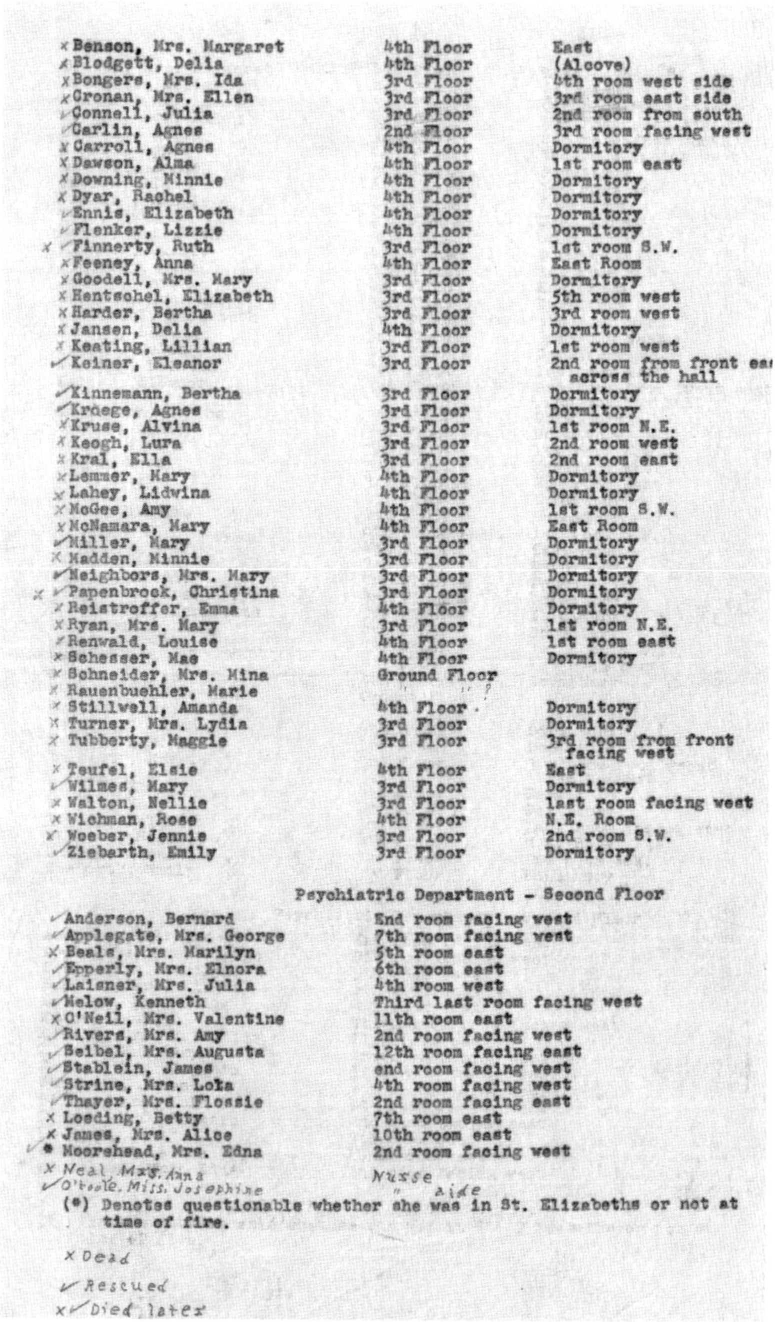

x	Benson, Mrs. Margaret	4th Floor	East
x	Blodgett, Delia	4th Floor	(Alcove)
x	Bongers, Mrs. Ida	3rd Floor	4th room west side
x	Cronan, Mrs. Ellen	3rd Floor	3rd room east side
✓	Connell, Julia	3rd Floor	2nd room from south
✓	Carlin, Agnes	2nd Floor	3rd room facing west
x	Carroll, Agnes	4th Floor	Dormitory
x	Dawson, Alma	4th Floor	1st room east
x	Downing, Minnie	4th Floor	Dormitory
x	Dyar, Rachel	4th Floor	Dormitory
✓	Ennis, Elizabeth	4th Floor	Dormitory
✓	Flenker, Lizzie	4th Floor	Dormitory
x ✓	Finnerty, Ruth	3rd Floor	1st room S.W.
x	Feeney, Anna	4th Floor	East Room
x	Goodell, Mrs. Mary	3rd Floor	Dormitory
x	Hentschel, Elizabeth	3rd Floor	5th room west
x	Harder, Bertha	3rd Floor	3rd room west
x	Jansen, Delia	4th Floor	Dormitory
x	Keating, Lillian	3rd Floor	1st room west
✓	Keiner, Eleanor	3rd Floor	2nd room from front east across the hall
✓	Kinnemann, Bertha	3rd Floor	Dormitory
✓	Kroege, Agnes	3rd Floor	Dormitory
x	Kruse, Alvina	3rd Floor	1st room N.E.
x	Keogh, Lura	3rd Floor	2nd room west
x	Kral, Ella	3rd Floor	2nd room east
x	Lemmer, Mary	4th Floor	Dormitory
x	Lahey, Lidwina	4th Floor	Dormitory
x	McGee, Amy	4th Floor	1st room S.W.
x	McNamara, Mary	4th Floor	East Room
✓	Miller, Mary	3rd Floor	Dormitory
x	Madden, Minnie	3rd Floor	Dormitory
✓	Neighbors, Mrs. Mary	3rd Floor	Dormitory
x ✓	Papenbrock, Christina	3rd Floor	Dormitory
x	Reistroffer, Emma	4th Floor	Dormitory
x	Ryan, Mrs. Mary	3rd Floor	1st room N.E.
x	Renwald, Louise	4th Floor	1st room east
x	Schesser, Mae	4th Floor	Dormitory
x	Schneider, Mrs. Mina	Ground Floor	
x	Rauenbuehler, Marie	'' '' ?	
x	Stillwell, Amanda	4th Floor	Dormitory
x	Turner, Mrs. Lydia	3rd Floor	Dormitory
x	Tubberty, Maggie	3rd Floor	3rd room from front facing west
x	Teufel, Elsie	4th Floor	East
✓	Wilmes, Mary	3rd Floor	Dormitory
x	Walton, Nellie	3rd Floor	last room facing west
x	Wichman, Rose	4th Floor	N.E. Room
x	Woeber, Jennie	3rd Floor	2nd room S.W.
✓	Ziebarth, Emily	3rd Floor	Dormitory

Psychiatric Department - Second Floor

✓	Anderson, Bernard	End room facing west
✓	Applegate, Mrs. George	7th room facing west
x	Beals, Mrs. Marilyn	5th room east
✓	Epperly, Mrs. Elnora	6th room east
✓	Laisner, Mrs. Julia	4th room west
✓	Melow, Kenneth	Third last room facing west
x	O'Neil, Mrs. Valentine	11th room east
✓	Rivers, Mrs. Amy	2nd room facing west
✓	Seibel, Mrs. Augusta	12th room facing east
✓	Stablein, James	end room facing west
✓	Strine, Mrs. Lota	4th room facing west
✓	Thayer, Mrs. Flossie	2nd room facing east
x	Loeding, Betty	7th room east
x	James, Mrs. Alice	10th room east
✓ *	Moorehead, Mrs. Edna	2nd room facing west
x	Neal, Mrs. Anna	Nurse
✓	O'Toole, Miss. Josephine	" aide

(*) Denotes questionable whether she was in St. Elizabeths or not at time of fire.

x Dead

✓ Rescued

x✓ Died later

This document was used to tally who had survived and who was taken victim by the fire—note the handwritten key at the bottom of the document. *Photo courtesy of the Davenport Fire Museum.*

the building once stood. All that was left was the corner of the foundation, scorched by flames, preserving the memory of that horrific night. As they walked quietly, they remembered their friends, sixteen of whom were laid to rest just feet from the building. Forty-one lives were lost that night, but so many lives were gravely affected and changed forever. The air was cold that morning, but the memories of that night of horror were bone-chilling.

CHAPTER 12

A FIREPROOF FUTURE

A great deal can be learned from the horrific events that took place on that cold early morning of January 7, 1950. Following any tragic event, it is imperative that changes be made and lessons learned to prevent history from repeating itself. Many of the suggested changes in structure safety and resources were summarized by R.E. McLain, manager of the Iowa Inspection Bureau, in the report he formulated titled *Mercy Hospital St. Elizabeth's Ward Building Fire*, which thoroughly detailed the building's conditions before the fire took place. The report concluded that there were six reasons the fire was as catastrophic as it was. Those reasons are included here in quotations, followed by analysis of how those conditions could be avoided in the future.

(1) "Delay in the discovery of the fire." What was clear following the thorough investigation was that Elnora started the fire inside a room only she was in sometime in the early morning hours of January 7, 1950. Best estimates are that fire was set to the curtains sometime between 1:45 and 2:00 a.m. The fire was first discovered by obstetric nurse Ellen Hilldebrand, who was working over at Mercy Hospital sometime after 2:00 a.m. Initially, Hilldebrand believed that the flashing lights she saw were coming from an ambulance arriving at the hospital, not a fire in one of its ward buildings. Hilldebrand passed the information to orderly Murray Francis, who then ran outside to see for himself.

After Murray Francis witnessed the blaze, he passed along the information for someone to call emergency personnel. He was told that this had already been done. It was 2:06 a.m. when the first alarm call reached Lieutenant Alvin Koranda at Engine No. 6. The time that had passed was likely between ten and twenty minutes. It is estimated that fires inside a facility or home double in size every thirty seconds and that three minutes into a fire, the room that was the source of the fire can climb to as high as five hundred degrees Fahrenheit. Within five minutes, it is believed, much of the opportunity for rescue would have passed due to the spread of the fire. Koranda reported that his men arrived around two minutes after the first alarm call went out, meaning that by the time the first firefighters arrived, the fire had been burning for at least twelve minutes.

The discovery of fire was improved with the invention and widespread implementation of home smoke detectors in 1965. These allowed for fires to be discovered faster and, importantly, within the time frame when rescue would still be possible.

(2) "Lack of a thoroughly organized program for evacuation of patients under emergency conditions." As it can be understood now, evacuation within the first few minutes is a vital part of preserving life and limiting the number of victims. St. Elizabeth's was a relatively understaffed unit, having only two nurses in the building at the time of the fire to cover the sixty-three patients who were residing there at the time. This greatly hindered their ability to prepare and carry out a plan that would efficiently get patients out in a timely manner. Considering that many of the patients were elderly and mentally ill, carrying out an evacuation plan would likely have been quite difficult.

Today, the United States Fire Administration (USFA) recommends having a map made available to all residents of a facility that details at least two possible ways of exiting in case of an emergency. St. Elizabeth's was equipped with two exits as well as a fire escape staircase. Due to the location of the fire, the fire escape was quickly involved, rendering one of those options unavailable. Doors that led to the two main staircases in the building were locked to keep people on their floors, keeping the forty-five residents on the third and fourth floors from being able to evacuate by themselves. Today, the USFA recommends as a part of your evacuation plan that doors and windows are not locked. At St. Elizabeth's, almost all windows and doors were locked at that time of night. This was an important factor that tragically led to such a gross loss of life.

(3) "Window bars and grilles of a type which could not readily be released from the outside." All the windows at St. Elizabeth contained iron bars, some of which included a lock-and-key mechanism. While the exact purpose

of the iron bars may not be fully understood, one suggestion is that they might have been installed as the result of an accident that took place in 1910. Twenty-seven-year-old Sophia Moeller was in Mercy Hospital being treated for appendicitis. After surgery on December 28, 1910, she became "delirious," according to hospital staff, and asked for the window to be opened to cool off the room. After then asking the nurse for an "ice cap," Moeller threw herself out of the fourth-floor window. She died as a result of her injuries two hours later. Early photographs of St. Elizabeth's show the building without iron bars covering the windows.

The fire code adopted in the 1990s requires that any building with iron bars on the windows has to have a quick-release mechanism in case of an emergency. Following the destruction of St. Elizabeth's, a large fundraising campaign was started to support the building of a fifty-bed mental health facility, this time without barred windows. It should be noted that bars on the windows of facilities such as St. Elizabeth's were not uncommon at the time. In fact, R.E. McClain stated in his report that the "conditions described in the report exist in many of the well managed and highly regarded institutions throughout the country." He went on to say, however, that "if remedial corrections can be secured, recurring fires with a high death toll may be avoided." This eventually would be true, as the number of deaths caused by fires since 1950 has been reduced by more than half, while the U.S. population has more than doubled.

(4) "Presence of an unusually large amount of combustible interior finish." Today, most of the materials used in our buildings—including furniture, building materials and fabrics—contain some type of flame-retardant chemical or other additive. This prevents fires from spreading quickly once they have started. On the contrary, the drapes that Elnora lit with the newspaper were highly flammable and gave the fire an unfair head start.

Once the heat increased near the source of the fire, the fire was allowed to spread horizontally with the help of four-foot-high wood wainscoting on the interior walls, beaverboard partitions, a fresh coat of interior paint completed in the fall and a suspended fiberboard ceiling that ran the entire length of the building. Vertically, the fire was allowed to spread with the assistance of wood lath and plaster walls that were secured to one-inch furring strips spanning the four floors, connecting each one to the next. In other constructions at this time, fire stops were put in place, limiting the spread of fire to rooms above or below the source. Fire stops fill openings inside walls that could otherwise allow smoke and fire to travel through.

(5) "The absence of fire stopping in the furring behind lath on exterior walls, old open vent flues with openings in each story and inadequate enclosure of floor openings." A fire needs oxygen, a heat source and fuel to maintain a constant burn. The previous section explains the fuel source: the building consisted of a large amount of combustible material. It is also known that Elnora used her husband's lighter as the source of heat for the fire. The last and final component was provided by the outdated design of the building. St. Elizabeth's contained two circulation vents on each floor, a dumbwaiter near the source and uncapped chimneys with openings to each floor.

To make matters worse, the dumbwaiter shaft, which was located adjacent to where Elnora started the fire, was lined on the inside with plasterboard and wood. Once fire entered the dumbwaiter, likely within a few minutes, it spread immediately to other floors and burned strongly. This helps explain why firemen Phillip Axelrod and Alvin Koranda entered the basement of the building and saw flames "shooting" out of the dumbwaiter. Fire never spread farther into the basement because it lacked combustible material.

(6) "Dependence upon one individual to handle an emergency, at the time of day when additional help is least available." One of the reasons for such a large loss from the fire, cited previously, was the lack of an evacuation program. While there were two staff members working on the night of the fire, one of them, night attendant Josephine O'Toole, was asleep in her third-floor bed when the fire broke out. This was a typical practice, as there were fewer needs among the patients during the overnight hours. That left all sixty-three patients and one other staff member all in the hands of nurse Anna Neal.

Another obvious disadvantage was the time of night the fire broke out in the building. The lack of foot and car traffic delayed the fire from being recognized until a number of minutes after it started. Communication was then passed from person to person until somebody called the emergency personnel. The fire alarm box, located about one hundred feet from the entrance, was never utilized.

When there is a fire in a building and lives are at stake, literally every minute is crucial to the outcome and mortality of the event. In hindsight, a number of measures could have been taken to ensure that an incident like a fire in a patient's room didn't turn into an emergency of this scale. Of those measures, more personnel to help signal emergency services while others were being led to safety and use of an emergency signaling device, like the fire alarm located outside of the building, would have likely saved more lives.

Gaining these critical seconds and minutes would have certainly led to a smaller number of casualties.

As far as the response of the fire department is concerned, Iowa Inspection Bureau manager R.E. McLain reported that the firefighting met and exceeded the expectations of the state. There was ample water supply surrounding the hospital campus, and hydrants were easily accessed. Only one hydrant didn't produce water, and this wasn't a significant factor. The fire department was well trained, responded in adequate time and had appropriate equipment for the task at hand. McLain concluded that "the fire department did their work well, but the task of rescuing patients and controlling the fire would have been an almost hopeless operation for any fire department."

While the report produced a great number of facts and conclusions, it can be difficult to point one solitary finger at any one area of weakness for the grave fatalities that took place. The State of Iowa and, in many ways, the entire country implemented the changes previously mentioned in large part due to tragedies like this one. The fire at St. Elizabeth's remains the deadliest fire in the history of Iowa, and it certainly received the attention at the time that it deserved. News outlets all over the globe reported about the fire, making it more obvious to the public that sometimes the unimaginable does indeed happen. With the modifications to building standards that we see today, it has been made possible that this type of tragedy doesn't receive an encore.

Lives were lost due to a great deal of reasons, some structural, some logistical and others more human. Communities today expect more out of their municipalities. Improvements to building structures and fire safety are just two of those expectations. Others include bettering the treatment of those who are mentally ill, treating patients based on severity of their condition and not the stigma associated with its symptoms, treating people of different backgrounds with dignity and respect and coming together as communities to create something better for everyone.

And that's exactly what eventually happened in Davenport, Iowa. Following the completion of the investigation, the Davenport community raised over $1 million to fund the building of a new mental health wing that would be added to Mercy Hospital. It would have better resources, better facilities and better care. One important note on the structure of the new building—it would be completely fireproof.

This gives the highlights of a night of horror, and I pray to God that no other fire department is ever called upon to face a similar situation.

—Davenport fire chief Lester Schick

CHAPTER 13

MORE THAN JUST NAMES

Marilyn Veronica (Collins) Beals: Beals was born August 27, 1922, in Rock Island, Illinois, to Frank and Josephine Collins. She married William Beals in Belleville, Illinois, in 1943, and together they had a son, William Jr., in 1947. They lived at 2001 Sixteenth Street in Rock Island, Illinois—about two blocks north of Rock Island High School. Marilyn had been receiving treatment at St. Elizabeth's on and off for five weeks after suffering what her doctor called "delayed shock" as a result of an automobile accident that took place on October 18, 1949. Her doctor, John Marker, said she was in "great condition" and would call home daily to check on her son, Billy. She was scheduled to be released from the hospital on the day of the fire. Marilyn was the patient Elnora went to wake after she started the fire, but for unknown reasons, she did not follow Elnora out of the building. Her room was on the first floor of the building, directly next to Elnora's. When her body was found, it had been burned beyond recognition. Dr. Marker, identified her by the rings she still had on her fingers. She was twenty-seven years old at the time of her tragic death. Her son was set to celebrate his third birthday just ten days later. Marilyn is buried in Calvary Cemetery in her home city of Rock Island, Illinois.

Margaret "Maggie" Benson: Margaret (Kelly) Benson was born in Jackson County, Iowa, in February 1877 to Timothy and Mary Jane Kelly, both Irish Catholic immigrants. She was the sixth of their seven children. Maggie went on to get married and have two children. She entered care at

St. Elizabeth's around 1909, living the last forty-one years of her life in the institution. Her room was on the east side of the fourth floor in the common dormitory. She received her treatment from Dr. Donohoe while at St. Elizabeth's. Maggie was one of the sixteen women considered "unclaimed and/or unidentifiable" and is buried at the Sacred Heart Cemetery. She was seventy-two years old at the time of her death.

Della Blodgett: Della was born in 1883 in Burlington, Iowa, to William and Ida Blodgett. Her father died before she was even two years old, leaving her mother to raise her. She married Henry Schmidt in 1910, and together, they had two children. One of those children, John Henry, died within twenty-four hours of his birth in 1915. Della and Henry conceived their second son, Earl Robert, in 1918; he died when he was only two years old in 1921. Della filed for and was granted a divorce from her husband in March 1923. She was considered a county patient, meaning the county was in charge of her care. While at St. Elizabeth's, her bed was near the alcove on the fourth floor of the building. Her treatment was given under the supervision of Dr. Donohoe. Della was one of the sixteen women considered "unclaimed and/or unidentifiable" and is buried at the Sacred Heart Cemetery. Her death certificate, issued by coroner Wildman, lists her birth year incorrectly as 1902 and does not include any date. In the area typically reserved for the signature of a family witness, the words "Records of Mercy Hospital" are printed. At the time of her death, Della was sixty-seven years old.

Ida Theresa Bongers: Ida was born June 20, 1865, in Keokuk, Iowa, to Anthony and Anna Faber. She married Anthony Bongers in 1884, and together they had two sons, including the Reverend Herman V. Bongers. Reverend Bongers was a former assistant pastor at St. Paul the Apostle church in Davenport and later became the chaplain at both Mercy Hospital and the Veterans Domiciliary, both in Clinton, Iowa. His first assignment after graduating from St. Ambrose College in Davenport was to serve as chaplain for the state prison in Ft. Madison, Iowa. Prior to entering care at St. Elizabeth's, Ida was a resident of Ottumwa, Iowa. She was a member of St. Patrick's Catholic Church there as well as an active member of the Altar and Rosary Society. While Ida was at St. Elizabeth's, her room was on the west side of the building on the third floor. She was under the care of Dr. Donohoe. Ida was buried in the Calvary Cemetery in Ottumwa. She was eighty-four years old when she died.

AGNES CARROL: Agnes Carroll was born in Peoria, Illinois, in 1897 to Thomas and Jane Carroll. Not a great deal is known about her life, but she entered St. Elizabeth's sometime prior to 1925, when she was in her early twenties. Agnes was one of the seventeen individuals who died that lived on the fourth-floor dormitory of the mental health ward. She was cared for by Dr. Donohoe. Her body was never discovered; she is considered one of the "unclaimed and or unidentified" victims and is memorialized at the Sacred Heart Cemetery. She was fifty-two years old when she died.

ELLA CRONIN: Ella Cronin was born in Indiana to Michael Cronin and Johanna Hayes around 1860. Census records suggest that she had been at St. Elizabeth's for more than thirty years. Reports indicate that Ella's body was never found after the fire. Records for Ella are scarce, with all reports of her from newspapers mistakenly listing her as "Ellen Cronan." Her room at St. Elizabeth's was on the third floor on the east side, almost directly above where the fire was started. The care that she received was under the direction of Dr. Donohoe. She was one of the sixteen women considered "unclaimed and/or unidentifiable" and is buried at the Sacred Heart Cemetery. Ella was eighty-nine years old when she died in the fire.

ALMA DAWSON: Records on Alma Dawson are somewhat limited. She was born Alma Lulu Curran in 1870 in Washington, Iowa, and was married to Cashius Dawson. In the early to mid-1910s, Cashius fought to give up guardianship of Alma and transfer it to someone else, essentially wiping his hands clean of any association with his spouse. Alma was first taken into custody by the county on January 27, 1910, after her husband complained that she was mentally ill. A hearing was held before the "commissioners of insanity," and it was determined that she met their criteria. She was admitted to St. Elizabeths at that time. Alma's siblings took control of her assets and throughout her stay at St. Elizabeth's would sell her belongings, including plots of land, to help with treatment costs. Her room at St. Elizabeth's was on the fourth floor on the east side of the building; by the time most firemen arrived, fire was already coming out of this section of the building. Alma was one of the sixteen women considered "unclaimed and/or unidentifiable" and is buried at the Sacred Heart Cemetery, just feet from where the tragic fire burned. She was seventy-nine years old when she died.

MINNIE DOWNING: Minnie Downing was born on October 19, 1873, to Henry and Sophie Langwerth (Thielman) in Davenport, Iowa. Minnie married Harry Downing in Clinton, Iowa, in June 1900. Harry was an immigrant from west central England. In June 1902, the Scott County Board of Insanity commissioners gathered and found that Minnie met the criteria for being considered "insane." She had been receiving care from Mercy Hospital for some time leading up to that. It was said that she was "suffering from a hallucination that her luck had all left her since she married." In an effort to "retrieve the luck," Minnie made habitual visits to fortune tellers, seeking their help. She was committed to Mount Pleasant Insane Asylum for treatment and later moved to St. Elizabeth's. In 1916, the county took over her care, meaning it would pay for any treatment she received. This was common for mental health patients at the time, as many of them had few family members who would stay involved and even fewer willing to contribute financially. Minnie was a resident of St. Elizabeth's for nearly forty years, staying on the fourth floor in the dormitory. She received treatment under Dr. Donohoe. Minnie was one of the sixteen women considered "unclaimed and/or unidentifiable" and is buried at the Sacred Heart Cemetery. She was seventy-six years old when she died.

RACHEL (MCDANIEL) DYAR: Rachel Dyar was born on May 12, 1866, to Mr. and Mrs. Joseph McDaniel just outside of Soldiers Grove, Wisconsin. Rachel grew up with ten siblings and lived on a farm in rural Wisconsin. She got married in 1913 to Finley Dyar and, shortly after, moved to North Dakota with her husband. After about fifteen years, she moved down to Davenport, Iowa, and would live the rest of her life there. She was a well-known resident of St. Elizabeth's hospital, where she spent the last ten years of her life. Rachel was one of the many patients being overseen by Dr. Donohoe. Her room was located on the fourth floor of the hospital, a floor that was originally intended as an attic but had been converted into a dormitory. After her death, her body was returned to rural Wisconsin, where she was buried at Mount Tabor Cemetery in Sabin. She was eighty-three years old at the time of her death.

ANNA FEENEY: Anna Feeney was born January 10, 1875, to Patrick Feeney and Sarah Gillon in Davenport, Iowa. Anna was never married and had no children. She was a lifelong member of the Sacred Heart parish in Davenport. She lived most of her life at 809 East Sixth Street in the east end of downtown Davenport. Anna had been a patient of St. Elizabeth's for around nine years when she died. Her room was on the east side of the fourth floor. Care given to Anna was under the supervision of Dr. Donohoe. She was one of the sixteen women considered "unclaimed and/or unidentifiable" and is buried at the Sacred Heart Cemetery. While her obituary only states that she was "about 70" when she died, Feeney was three days short of her seventy-fifth birthday when the fire took her life.

FLORENCE MARGARET "MARY" GOODELL: Florence "Mary" Goodell was born on August 4, 1871, in Chicago, Illinois, to John and Maggie Robinson. In 1895, she married Ray J. Goodell in LaSalle, Illinois, and together they had two children, William and Elroy. In 1911, the family moved to Davenport, Iowa, and resided at 2002 Gaines Street. Ray died in 1943 of kidney failure. Mary was an active member of the Trinity Episcopal church as well as Royal Neighbors. She had been a patient of St. Elizabeth's for about ten years prior to the fire, under the supervision of Dr. Donohoe. Mary's room was located on the third floor. Her remains were never discovered after the fire, and she is memorialized as one of the sixteen "unclaimed and/or unidentified" at the Sacred Heart Cemetery near the hospital grounds. Mary was seventy-nine when she died.

BERTHA HARDER: Bertha Harder was born on April 17, 1868, to Mr. and Mrs. Michael Musal. She was a German immigrant whose family moved to the United States when she was young and settled in the Quad City area. Bertha married George Harder in Davenport in 1883, and he would precede her in death. Together they had six children, five sons and one daughter. Bertha was a resident of Davenport prior to entering St. Elizabeth's in 1940. Her room was located on the third floor of St. Elizabeth's. Besides her six children, she also left behind eight grandchildren and seven great-grandchildren. Her body was buried in the Maysville Cemetery, a few minutes northwest of the Quad Cities. She was eighty-two years old at the time of her death.

ELIZABETH HENTSCHEL: Elizabeth Hentschel was born in Germany on April 26, 1863. She immigrated to the United States on March 18, 1894, arriving in New York City. Immigration documents suggest that she was a petite, brown-haired, blue-eyed woman. Elizabeth was cared for by Dr. Donahoe and had a room on the third floor that was rather centrally located inside the building. At the time of her death, Elizabeth had no known relatives to contact. Her death certificate reads "the records of Mercy Hospital" in the place where an informant would sign. She is buried in the Mount Calvary

Catholic cemetery in Davenport, Iowa. Elizabeth Hentschel was eighty-seven years old when she died in the fire.

Alice James: Alice Lila James was born on July 27, 1873, to John and Helen Maria McCann in Cedar County, Iowa. She married Archibald James in March 1907 in Muscatine, Iowa. Together, they were very social people who enjoyed local theater and frequently held gatherings at their home for family. Alice was the last patient to arrive at the hospital before the fire, having been admitted on Friday, January 6, at eight o'clock in the evening. Alice was set to be cared for by Dr. Marker in her time at St. Elizabeth's. Her room was located on the east side of the main floor, close to the northeast exit. Her family presumed she was still missing from the fire until her body was positively identified on Monday, January 9, at a nearby funeral home. She is buried in the Oak Ridge Cemetery in West Liberty, Iowa. She was seventy-seven years old at the time of her death.

Della Marie (Moltzen) Jensen: Della Jensen was born on on July 27, 1883, in Omaha, Nebraska, to Henry and Minnie Moltzen. In 1928, Della married Carl A. Jensen in Clinton, Iowa. She was sent to St. Elizabeth's for treatment in 1933 when she was fifty years old and was a resident there until her death. She resided on the fourth floor in the common dormitory with other patients and was receiving care under Dr. Donohoe. Her funeral was held on Tuesday, January 10, 1950, at McGinnis Funeral Home, with the Reverend J.A. Miller officiating. She was buried at Oakdale Cemetery in Davenport. She was sixty-six years old when she died.

Lillie Keating: Lillie Keating was a lifelong Davenport resident who was born on July 7, 1865. She was raised by her parents, Clark and Margaret Hall. She was widowed after losing her husband, Bernard M. Keating, who died over thirty years prior to her. Together, they had two surviving children, Ellen and Bernard Jr. They spent many years raising their children in the heart of Davenport at their home on Perry Street. While at St. Elizabeth's, Lillie's room was the first on the third floor, with a good view of the main hospital. Her physician was Dr. Donohoe. Lillie's funeral was held at Halligan Funeral Home, followed by a requiem high mass at Sacred Heart Cathedral in Davenport. She is buried at the Holy Family Cemetery in Davenport. She was eighty-four years old at the time of her death.

Lura Keogh: Lura Keogh was born on February 1, 1870, to William and Lura (Benjamin) Keogh in Ireland; shortly thereafter, her family immigrated to the United States. Keogh was a proud Catholic and was very devout in her faith. She never married and had been a resident of St. Elizabeth for the last fifty years, entering for treatment while in her late twenties. Her room was located on the third floor of St. Elizabeth's, next to Lillie Keating. She was buried in Mt. Olivet cemetery in Chicago, Illinois. Her brother, prominent heart surgeon Dr. Chester H. Keogh of Chicago, was her only known surviving relative. Ironically, records indicate that relics from the Chicago Fire of 1871 were stored in his Chicago home. Lura Keogh was seventy-nine years old at the time of her death.

Ellen "Ella" Rosena Kral: Ella Kral was born on April 2, 1877, in Hills, Iowa, to George Mentzer and Caroline Feldman. She married Adam Kral in November 1900, and together they lived on a farm south of Iowa City for the majority of their lives. Together they had three children, who all continued to live near them in Hills, Iowa. She was admitted to St. Elizabeth's sometime after 1940. Her room was located on the third floor on the east side, very close to where the fire was initially started. The treatment given to her was under the supervision of Dr. Donohoe. Ella's remains were never identified after the fire, though she is memorialized at the grave site in the Sacred Heart Cemetery on the campus of Mercy Hospital. A private funeral mass took place with her family at the St. Joseph's Church in Hills nine days later. All three of her children and her husband were in attendance. She was seventy-two years old at the time of her death.

Alvina Kruse: Alvina was one of five children born to August and Magdalena Kruse. She was born and lived her entire life in Davenport, with her last known personal address at 822 West Locust Street. Alvina's family had a history of mental illness; her mother committed suicide in October 1936. At the time, Alvina was living with her then eighty-eight-year-old mother, who had been threatening to take her own life. After Alvina felt confident that she had talked her out of doing anything drastic, her mother went missing. Alvina went out to the backyard and found her mother's body at the bottom of a twelve-foot water well, in about four feet of water. She had jumped to her death. It is certainly reasonable to conclude that the trauma of finding her deceased mother contributed to her mental illness. The tragedy of her mother's suicide also draws a strong connection to the history of mental illness in her family. Alvina also lost her sister Adella, who passed away after a long illness when Alvina was forty-six years old. Alvina's room was located in the northeast corner of the third floor of the ward. She is buried in the Fairmount Cemetery in west Davenport. Alvina was a few weeks shy of her eighty-fifth birthday when she died.

LIDWINA M. LAHEY: Lidwina Lahey was born on September 26, 1897, to Daniel Lahey and Mary Hand in Clinton, Iowa. Fifteen months later, her parents brought home another child, her younger brother, Raymond. The family of four lived with Lidwina's maternal grandparents near downtown Clinton. Her mother, Mary, died when Lidwina was only thirteen years old. Lidwina was never married and had no children. Instead, in her late twenties or early thirties, she entered into the Mount Alverno Home, a rehabilitation center that had a mental health unit. She was then moved to St. Elizabeth in 1938 to receive a more skilled level of care. Her room was on the fourth-floor dormitory, making it nearly impossible for her to get out on the night of the fire. Lidwina was cared for under the supervision of Dr. Donohoe. Her body was taken to McGinnis Funeral Home, where her younger brother, Raymond, attempted to identify her remains. Her body had been badly burned but was accepted by the family as being Lidwina's. She is buried in the Calvary Cemetery in the north end of her hometown in Clinton. Lidwina was fifty-three years old when she died in the fire.

MARY FRANCES LEMMER: Mary Lemmer was born in Cedar Falls, Iowa, on March 1, 1886, to John and Elizabeth Lemmer. As a youth, Mary attended a boarding school in Clinton, Iowa, named Our Lady of Angels. As an adult, she was a devout member of the St. Patrick's Catholic Church in Cedar Falls. Her funeral service was held at that church on January 12, 1950. She had been a patient at St. Elizabeth's since 1930, when she was admitted at forty-four years old. Her room was located on the fourth floor of the building in the dormitory. She was identified in the aftermath of the fire by a recognizable ring that was still on her finger—the remainder of her body had been badly burned. Mary was sixty-four years old when she died in the fire.

ELIZABETH "BETTY" MARILYN LOEDING: Betty Loeding was born on July 11, 1927, in Davenport. Prior to her admission to St. Elizabeth's hospital, she was a resident of Monmouth, Iowa. She graduated from Davenport High School before continuing her education at American Institute of Commerce.

Betty Loeding's Davenport High School yearbook photo, taken just a few years prior to her death. *Photo courtesy of Ancestry.*

Betty worked as a secretary at the Masonic Temple before her mental illness. She was a state-admitted patient, meaning she was committed to the hospital by recommendation of the state. Prior to coming to St. Elizabeth's, Betty had been a patient at Mount Pleasant State Hospital. She was one of the six patients receiving care from Dr. Werner M. Hollander, the same doctor who admitted Elnora Epperly for treatment. Betty was the only one of his six patients to die in the fire. Her room was also located next to Elnora's, on the first floor of the building. She is buried in the Fairmount Cemetery in west Davenport. At the time of the fire, she was only twenty-two years old.

MARY "MINNIE" MADDEN: Minnie Madden was born on July 31, 1871, near Ottawa, Illinois. She was later married to Edward "Ted" Madden on April 24, 1900, in Lasalle, Illinois. Together they had six children, four sons and two daughters. Minnie's body was found near Maggie Tubberty's and Mary Ryan's on the south end of the third floor, near the fire escape. Minnie was being treated under the supervision of Dr. Donohoe. One of her daughters, Marie, was her legal guardian while she was in the hospital. Minnie's funeral took place at St. Francis Catholic church in Ottawa, Illinois. She was seventy-nine years old at the time of her death.

AMY MCGEE: Amy McGee was born on August 16, 1889, in Davenport, Iowa, to John McGee and Lovina Morgan. She would spend her entire life in the city of Davenport, alongside most of her family. Her body was moved to Runge Funeral Home but was so badly burned that it was unrecognizable. Her death certificate has "Unidentified Body Possibly" printed on it under the name section, with "Amy McGee" written next to it. It is believed that she had been a patient of St. Elizabeth's for about eight years. She was considered a county patient, meaning she was there at the order of the county, which paid for all treatments. Her bed was located in the southwest corner of the fourth-floor dormitory. The treatment she received while at St. Elizabeth's was done by Dr. Donohoe. Amy was one of the sixteen women considered "unclaimed and/or unidentifiable" and is buried at the Sacred Heart Cemetery. She was sixty years old at the time of her death.

MARY MCNAMARA: Mary McNamara was born on March 2, 1876, on a farm outside of Minonk, Illinois, to Michael McNamara and Mary Kelly. While at the institution, her bed was on the east side of the fourth-floor dormitory. She received care at the facility from Dr. Donohoe. Her sister-in-law Grace McNamara traveled to Davenport from Dekalb, Illinois, to identify her body and sign the death certificate. Her body was kept at Horrigan Funeral Home for identification before she was transferred back near her birthplace in Minonk. She is buried in St. Patrick's Catholic Cemetery, near the St. Patrick's Catholic Church where she was a member. Mary was seventy-three years old when she died.

ANNA (RANG) NEAL: Anna Neal was born in Euskirchen, Germany, on May 8, 1894. She was married twice; her first marriage was to Hermann W. Miller in 1920 until his death on January 8, 1926. She later married Albert B. Neal in June 1949 and was married to him until her death. Working as a nurses' aide who typically covered the night shift, Neal was the only employee of the hospital to die in the fire. Her body was found in the second room from the front door on the main floor of the building by first assistant

IOWA STATE DEPARTMENT OF HEALTH
Division of Vital Statistics
CERTIFICATE OF DEATH
STATE OF IOWA
Birth No. 01700
State File No. 82C-5-0 28

1. PLACE OF DEATH a. County: Scott
b. City or Town: Davenport
c. Length of Stay (in this place): 28 Yrs
d. Full Name of Hospital or Institution: Mercy Hospital
2. USUAL RESIDENCE a. State: Iowa b. County: Scott
c. City or Town: Davenport
d. Street Address: 729 Western Ave.
3. NAME OF DECEASED (Type or Print) a. (First): Anna b. (Middle) c. (Last): Neal
4. Date of Death: Jan 7 1950
5. Sex: Female
6. Color or Race: White
7. Married, Never Married, Widowed, Divorced (Specify): Married
8. Date of Birth: May 8, 1894
9. Age (In years last birthday): 55
10a. Usual Occupation: Nurses Aid
10b. Kind of Business or Industry: Mercy Hospital
11. Birthplace (State or foreign country): Eiusch Kirchen, Germany
12. Citizen of What Country? U.S.A.
13. Father's Name: Joseph Rang
14. Mother's Maiden Name: Mary Von Brook
15. Was Deceased Ever in U.S. Armed Forces? No
16. Social Security No.: None
17. Informant's Signature: Albert B. Neal
18. Cause of Death — MEDICAL CERTIFICATION
I. Disease or Condition Directly Leading to Death (a): Died in fire at St. Elizabeth Hosp.
Due to (b): Davenport, Iowa.
Interval Between Onset and Death: 1-7-50
II. Other Significant Conditions
19a. Date of Operation 19b. Major Findings of Operation
20. Autopsy? Yes ☐ No ☐
21a. Accident, Suicide, Homicide (Specify) 21b. Place of Injury 21c. (City, Town, or Township) (County) (State)
21d. Time of Injury 21e. Injury Occurred While at work ☐ Not while at work ☐ 21f. How Did Injury Occur?
22. I hereby certify that I attended the deceased from As Coroner 19__, to 1/7/ 1950, that I last saw the deceased alive on ____, 19__, and that death occurred at ____m., from the causes and on the date stated above.
23a. Attendant's Signature: [signature] Coroner
23b. Address: 1307 Robeson, Bettendorf, I.
23c. Date Signed: 1-9-50
24a. Burial, Cremation, Removal (Specify): Burial
24b. Date: 1/9/50
24c. Name of Cemetery or Crematory: Pine Hill Cem.
24d. Location: Davenport, Iowa
25. Funeral Director's Signature: [signature] Address: 824 W. 3rd St. Davenport, Iowa License Number: 1687
26. Date Rec'd by Local Registrar: 2-2-50
Registrar's Signature: [signature]
File Number: 53

Opposite: This funeral service mass was offered for Margaret Tubberty at St. John's Catholic Church in Davenport, beginning a string of funerals that would take place over the coming days. *Photo courtesy of the Davenport Public Library.*

Above: The death certificate for Anna Neal, shown here, played a large role in the criminal investigation following the fire at St. Elizabeth's. *Photo courtesy of Ancestry.*

fire chief Walter Schroeder. It is likely that this was the room of Marilyn Beal, who also perished in the fire. "She died a hero's death," one fireman said. Assistant Chief Schroeder and Lieutenant Williams carried Neal out of the front door of the building, through the porch and down the front stairs, where five or six Sisters recognized her and said, "Oh, it's Mrs. Neal." She was taken to Mercy Hospital, where Dr. Robert J. Neufeld, the same physician who attended to Elnora's wounded hand, pronounced her dead. "I put a stethoscope up to her chest and said she was dead," Dr. Nuefeld would later report to the county attorney. He relayed that he could see burns to her chest and face when he pronounced her dead but didn't assess her any further. After removal from the scene, her body was taken to Runge Mortuary and later buried next to that of her first husband, Hermann, in Pine Hill Cemetery. Her funeral took place at Zion Lutheran Church in Davenport, Iowa, where she was a member of the congregation. She was fifty-five years old at the time of her death.

Valentine O'Niell: Valentine O'Niell was born on April 18, 1890, to August Anthony and Mary Vandevorde in Rock Island, Illinois. She first married William Thurwanger, a German immigrant, in 1910. Together they had two children. Her husband died in 1922 at the age of thirty-seven. She then remarried, five years later, to Clement O'Niell in October 1927 in Kewanee, Illinois. Together, they had one son, James O'Niell. Her room was located on the second floor of St. Elizabeth's, on the east side toward the back of the building. Valentine was a patient under the care of Dr. Donohoe. Her body was taken back to Kewanee, where funeral services were held. She is buried there in the Mt. Olivet Cemetery. She was sixty years old when she died in the fire.

Marie Rauembuehler: Marie was born on December 22, 1895, to Carl and Anna Rauembuehler in West Point, Iowa, just outside of Burlington. She had been a patient at St. Elizabeth's for six years by the time of the fire. Prior to going to St. Elizabeth's Hospital for treatment, she lived on a farm in Pleasant Ridge Township, about twenty miles west of Burlington, with her brother Clem's family. Her room at St. Elizabeth's was on the fourth floor, suggesting that her illness was less severe than most patients'. The physician supervising her care was Dr. Donohoe. She is buried in West Point, Iowa, at the Calvary Cemetery, sharing a headstone with her siblings Clem, Anna and Leon. She was fifty-four years old at the time of her death.

Emma Reistroffer: Emma was born in June 1877 in Davenport, Iowa, to Henry Millhouse and Susan Schrader. She married Frank Traeger in September 1908 in Davenport. Frank died on December 4, 1921, as a result of a hemorrhagic stroke. Emma went on to marry a farmer, Anthony Reistroffer, on December 1, 1922. Emma's bed was located on the fourth floor of St. Elizabeth's. The medical treatment she received while there was done by Dr. Donohoe. Her remains were never found, and therefore, she was considered "missing and presumed dead." Emma is honored at the Sacred Heart Cemetery. She was seventy-two at the time of her death.

Mary "Louisa" Renwald: Louisa Renward was born in Summitville, Iowa, on February 23, 1872, to Jacob Renwald and Elizabeth Seibert. She was born into a large family; her parents had at least seven children. While at St. Elizabeth's, her room was located in the southeast corner of the fourth floor. She was cared for by Dr. Donohoe. Her older brother George also happened to be a patient at the male counterpart facility, St. John's, on the night of the fire. Another one of her older brothers, John Henry, died less than four weeks after Louisa. A large family gathering was held at the Renwald home to remember John. Louisa's body, on the contrary, was never identified, and instead, she was one of the sixteen victims buried in the Sacred Heart Cemetery on the grounds of the hospital. She was seventy-seven years old at the time of her death.

Mary Ryan: Mary Ryan was born to Stephen and Mary Mills in Fulton County in western Illinois on April 6, 1867. She was the daughter of a farmer and lived in a large family with seven other siblings. At the time of her death, newspapers reported that she "had family in Avon, IL," which is in Fulton County. She spent the last twenty-two years of her life at St. Elizabeth's, with her room located on the third floor of the building. Mary had very little family when she passed, with her legal guardian being her nephew, Stephen Mills. She is buried just north of Avon, Illinois, at the Saint Augustine Cemetery, a small rural cemetery in the country. She was eighty-two years old when she died in the fire.

Elsie Teuful: Elsie was born on November 15, 1898, in Victor, Iowa to parents Alois and Wilhemina Teuful. Her father, Alois, was a German immigrant who married Wilhemina after meeting her in New York. Elsie was never married but was beloved by family, as evidenced by her headstone, which reads "Aunt Elsie A. Teuful." Elsie had been a resident at St. Elizabeth's for over ten years prior to the fire. Her room was listed as "4th Floor East," suggesting that somewhat of a makeshift room had been put together. She was one of the seventeen to die on the fourth floor, with only two from the "dormitory" surviving the fire. She was buried back home in Victor, Iowa, in the Calvary Cemetery. Elsie Teuful was fifty-one years old at the time of her death.

Margaret "Maggie" Tubberty: Maggie Tubberty was born in October 1863 in Winona, Minnesota, to Patrick and Catherine Tubberty, both of whom were Irish immigrants. When Maggie was young, her family moved

Scott County Highway Department workers were brought in to dig the sixteen graves just north of Mercy Hospital that were necessary to bury those who were unidentified and unclaimed. *Photo courtesy of the Davenport Public Library.*

to Davenport, Iowa, where she and her brother John were raised. Margaret spent fifteen years of her life serving as the housekeeper for the Reverend T.P. Coleman, who was pastor of Our Lady of Lourdes Catholic Church in nearby Bettendorf, Iowa. Reverend Coleman was the officiant at her funeral, which was held at St. Mary's Catholic Church in Davenport. Maggie was a former resident of McAuley Hall, a care facility also started by the Sisters of Mercy at Eighth and Fillmore Streets in Davenport. Margaret's body was found in a room with those of Minnie Madden and Mary Ryan on the third floor at the south end of the building. This would have placed them on the floor above the fire, near the fire exit but with little chance of escape. Hospital records indicate that all three indeed had rooms on the third floor. Maggie had been a patient of Dr. Donohoe. She was buried in Davenport's Holy Family Cemetery with her parents on January 10, 1950. She was eighty-five years old when she died.

MARY "MAE" SCHESSER: Mae was born in 1882 in Davenport, Iowa, to Thomas O'Shaunghnessy and Catherine Orman. She was married to John Schesser in April 1919. John died in September 1949, a few months before

Mae's death. She first entered St. Elizabeth's in 1926 and lived there until her death. Her bed was located in the fourth-floor dormitory. Treatment for Mae was rendered by Dr. Donohoe. Her remains were never positively identified, and she was therefore considered "unclaimed and/or unidentifiable." She is buried in the Sacred Heart Cemetery. She was sixty-seven years old at the time of her death.

Mina Marie Schneider: Mina Schneider was born on May 13, 1862, in Germany and immigrated to the United States in the 1890s. She and her husband, Christian Ludwig, had four children: one daughter, Sam (Hirschel) Schneider, and three sons, Arthur, Alfred and Kurt. She had been a resident of St. Elizabeth's for thirty-four years when she died. Her room was located on the second floor, making her one of only five women to die who lived on that floor. Mina was one of the sixteen women considered "unclaimed and/or unidentifiable" and is buried at the Sacred Heart Cemetery. She was ninety-seven years old when she died.

Amanda Jabens Stillwell: Amanda Stillwell was born on February 15, 1896, in Reinbeck, Iowa. Amanda was married to Charles Stillwell, and together they had two children, Blanche and Charles Jr. In May 1920, Amanda's

Withered flowers sit on the headstone that marks the graves of the sixteen unidentified individuals who perished in the fire. *Author's collection.*

husband, Charles, asked a judge to grant him a divorce, citing "cruelty" as a reason. He reported that Amanda "threatened serious injury to him on several occasions." He also asked for custody of their two children at the time of the court filings. That divorce was finalized in June 1920. In 1935, Amanda was admitted to St. Elizabeth's. She was receiving treatment under the direction of Dr. Donohoe and resided in the fourth-floor dormitory. Amanda Stillwell was buried in the Fairmount Cemetery in Davenport. She was fifty-three years old when she died.

LYDIA (HARRISON) TURNER: Lydia Turner was born on September 22, 1865, in Davenport, Iowa, and lived there her entire life. For the majority of her life, she lived at 1517 West Third Street, near downtown. She was an active member of the Catholic Women's League and served on the board of directors of the Davenport Catholic Charities. Lydia's room was located on the third floor of St. Elizabeth. Her funeral services were held at St. Mary's Catholic Church, and she was later buried in the Holy Family Cemetery in west Davenport. Lydia Turner was eighty-four years old when she died.

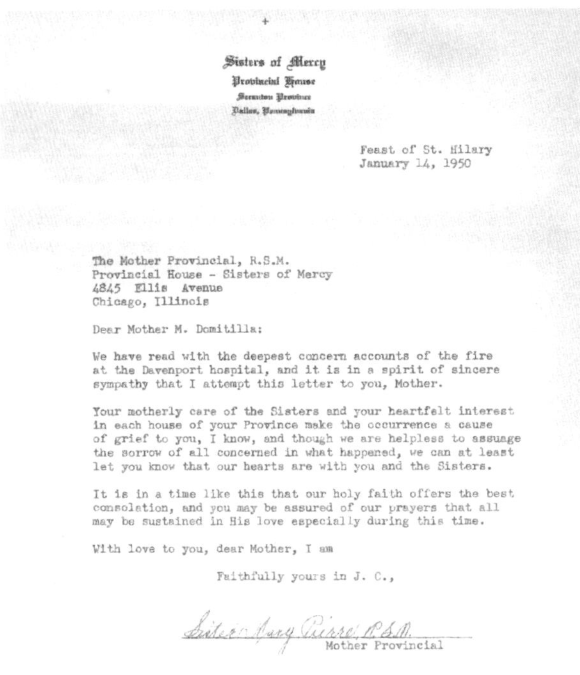

+

Sisters of Mercy
Provincial House
Scranton Province
Dallas, Pennsylvania

Feast of St. Hilary
January 14, 1950

The Mother Provincial, R.S.M.
Provincial House - Sisters of Mercy
4845 Ellis Avenue
Chicago, Illinois

Dear Mother M. Domitilla:

We have read with the deepest concern accounts of the fire at the Davenport hospital, and it is in a spirit of sincere sympathy that I attempt this letter to you, Mother.

Your motherly care of the Sisters and your heartfelt interest in each house of your Province make the occurrence a cause of grief to you, I know, and though we are helpless to assuage the sorrow of all concerned in what happened, we can at least let you know that our hearts are with you and the Sisters.

It is in a time like this that our holy faith offers the best consolation, and you may be assured of our prayers that all may be sustained in His love especially during this time.

With love to you, dear Mother, I am

Faithfully yours in J. C.,

Sister Mary Pierre, R.S.M.
Mother Provincial

Mother Provincial, an official who oversaw the Sisters of Mercy facilities in Davenport region, received a large number of letters and telegrams from across the country. *Photo courtesy of the Sisters of Mercy.*

NELLIE WALTON: Nellie Walton was born in Illinois in 1869. There are no records of her ever getting married, and census records suggest that she may have been single her whole life. When her death was reported in the papers, she was one of the few who didn't have a relative or an address listed. Records suggest she may have lived near Twelfth and Perry Streets in Davenport. She had been a resident of St. Elizabeth's for at least ten years by the time of the fire. The county took control over her guardianship in 1947. Her room was on the third floor, in the northwest corner of the building. She was cared for under the supervision of Dr. Donohoe. Nellie was one of the sixteen women considered "unclaimed and/or unidentifiable" and is buried at the Sacred Heart Cemetery. Nellie was ninety years old when she died in the fire.

ROSE "ROSA" WICHMAN: Rosa Wichman was born on February 27, 1875, in Steele, Indiana, to Anthony Wichman and Maria Kuhlman. Rosa was never married and never had any children. She entered the facility sometime before 1930 and was a resident there until she died, residing in the northeast corner of the fourth floor. She was cared for while at St. Elizabeth's by Dr. Donohoe. Rosa was one of the sixteen women considered "unclaimed and/or unidentifiable" and is buried at the Sacred Heart Cemetery. She was seventy-four years old at the time of her death.

MARGARET JANE "JENNIE" WOEBER: Jennie Woeber died at the hospital on Saturday, January 7, 1950, at 5:22 p.m. after being carried out of the building during the fire that morning. She survived around fifteen hours after having been rescued but eventually succumbed to her death as a result of shock and smoke inhalation. Woeber was St. Elizabeth's oldest resident and had been there for thirty years. She is buried in the Holy Family Cemetery on the west end of Davenport. She was ninety-three years old at the time of her death.

BIBLIOGRAPHY

Ancestry. Family Tree, Genealogy & Family History Records. https://www.ancestry.com.

Condon, Sister Mary Brigid. *From Simplicity to Elegance: The Story of Mercy Hospital, 1869–1994*. Davenport, IA: Genesis Health System Heart of Mercy Foundation, 1997.

Daily Times. "Deaths Set at 37 in Hospital Fire; 31 Bodies Recovered from Ruins." January 7, 1950.

———. "Fate Stepped In." January 7, 1950.

———. "Fire Probe Opens; Toll Rises to 40." January 9, 1950.

———. "Friends Tell of Mrs. Anna Neal's Prophecies." January 13, 1950.

———. "Testimony Backs Confession, Say Officials of Report." January 25, 1950.

———. "12 Dead Taken from St. Elizabeth's Fire Ruins; Casualties May Total 30." January 7, 1950.

———. "Woman Will Face Court in Deaths at Hospital Fire." January 13, 1950.

Davenport Fire Museum. "Scott County Coroner's Inquest." 1950.

Grimes, Bret, and Roy Porter. "Interview of Davenport Fireman." April 19, 2023. Davenport Fire Museum.

Harlan, Edgar Ruby. "The Irish in Iowa." In *A Narrative History of the People of Iowa*. Vol 3. Chicago: American Historical Society, 1931. www.celticcousins.net/irishiniowa/sistersofmercy.htm.

Loewy, Tom. "Firefighter, 95, Remembers Night of Horror at Davenport Hospital Fire, 70 Years Ago." *Quad-City Times*, January 6, 2020.

McLain, R.E. *Mercy Hospital St. Elizabeth's Ward Building Fire.* Des Moines: Iowa Inspection Bureau, 1950.

Mercy Hospital. Records. Davenport, IA.

Rogers, Kara. "Insulin Shock Therapy." *Encyclopædia Britannica*, May 26, 2023. www.britannica.com/science/insulin-shock-therapy.

Schricker, Mary. *The West End Kid: The Life of Doctor Jack Sunderbruch.* Davenport, IA: Doctor J.H. Sunderbruch Estate, 2007.

Sisters of Mercy. "Our History." https://sistersofmercy.org/about-us/our-history-mercy-heritage-center/.

Tueth, Michael J. "Schizophrenia: Emil Kraepelin, Adolph Meyer, and Beyond." *Journal of Emergency Medicine* 13, no. 6, 1995 (805–9). https://doi.org/10.1016/0736-4679(95)02022-5.

Wright-Mendoza, Jessie. "The (Unproven, Deadly) Common Cure for Schizophrenia." JSTOR Daily, November 2, 2018. https://daily.jstor.org/the-unproven-deadly-common-cure-for-schizophrenia/.

Wundrum, Bill. "Firefighter Witnessed Horrific 1950 Blaze." *Quad-City Times*, January 6, 2016.

INDEX

A

Axelrod, Phillip 44, 45, 47, 95, 102

B

Beals, Marilyn 37, 73, 84, 105
Benson, Maggie 105
Blodgett, Della 106
Bongers, Ida 106
Borremeo, Sister Elizabeth 22, 23

C

Carrol, Agnes 107
Carter, Donna 32, 79
Cox, Eileen 51, 53, 54, 55
Cronin, Ella 107

D

Dawson, Alma 107
Doss, Darrell 30, 49, 50, 95
Downing, Minnie 107, 108
Dyar, Rachel 74, 108

E

Epperly, John 31, 32, 81

F

Feeney, Anna 108, 109
Fee, Richard 60, 61, 62, 95
Filseth, Clark 85, 86, 87, 91, 93, 94, 96
Finnerty, Mary 68, 77
Francis, Murray 20, 41, 113

G

Gerdts, Harold 50, 51
Goodell, Mary 109

H

Harder, Bertha 109
Hentschel, Elizabeth 109
Hocke, Louis 48, 62
Hoeper, Ted 48, 62
Hollander, Werner 10, 11, 14, 31, 81, 82, 88, 94, 96, 112

J

James, Alice 29, 39, 56, 110, 116
Jensen, Della 110

K

Kalloway, Lucille 32, 33, 34, 36
Keating, Lillie 110, 111
Keogh, Lura 110, 111
Koranda, Alvin 44, 45, 46, 47, 48, 49, 56, 75, 95
Kral, Ella 111
Kruse, Alvina 74, 111

L

Lahey, Lidwina 112
Lange, Harry 43, 47, 48, 49, 51, 56, 95
Lemmer, Mary 112
Loeding, Betty 10, 112

M

Madden, Minnie 73, 113, 118
Marker, John 73, 85, 87, 88, 89, 90, 91, 92, 94, 105, 110
McGee, Amy 113
McNamara, Mary 74, 113

N

Neal, Anna 18, 34, 35, 36, 37, 50, 64, 65, 72, 84, 114, 123

O

O'Niell, Valentine 116
O'Toole, Josephine 18, 37, 38, 39, 48

P

Porter, Roy 5, 31, 57, 58, 59, 60, 67, 123

Q

Quinn, James 56, 95

R

Rauembuehler, Marie 74, 116
Reistroffer, Emma 116
Renwald, Louisa 116, 117
Rivera, Amy 57
Ryan, Mary 73, 113, 117, 118

S

Schesser, Mae 118
Schick, Lester 48, 49, 55, 56, 57, 58, 95
schizophrenia 124
Schneider, Mina 119
Second Alarmers 13, 57, 65
Stablein, James 39, 64, 76
Sternberg, Robert 44
Stillwell, Amanda 119
Sunderbruch, John 12, 13, 14, 61, 62, 95, 124

T

Teuful, Elsie 117
Tubberty, Maggie 73, 113, 117
Turner, Lydia 120

W

Walton, Nellie 120
Weinbrandt, Harry 81, 82, 83, 84, 85, 86
Wichman, Rosa 121
Wildman, C.H. 69, 70, 71, 72, 74, 106
Williams, Dwight 47, 48, 114
Woeber, Jane 65, 74, 121

ABOUT THE AUTHOR

Photo courtesy of Sarah Wagener.

Author Bret Grimes is an Illinois native and currently resides in the Quad Cities in eastern Iowa. In this book, he brings together his passion for preserving local history with his love of storytelling and preservation. Bret practices as a chiropractor in Bettendorf, where he lives with his wife and three children. This is his first book.